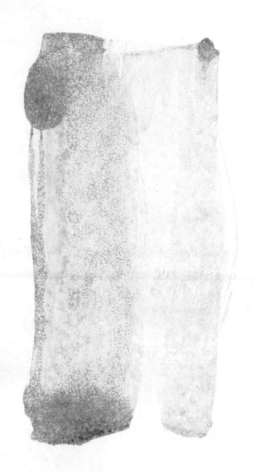

Love's Mysteries: the psychology of sexual attraction

Love's Mysteries: the psychology of sexual attraction

Glenn Wilson and David Nias

illustrations by Rick Cuff

Open Books

London

First published in 1976 by Open Books Publishing Limited,
87-89 Shaftesbury Avenue, LONDON W1V 7AD

© Glenn Wilson and David Nias 1976
ISBN 0 7291 0025 1

Filmset in Monophoto 11pt Photina by
Filmtype Services Ltd, Scarborough
Printed in Great Britain by
T. & A. Constable Ltd, Edinburgh

Contents

Acknowledgement

We would like to thank the authors and publishers of the book and articles from which illustrations and data have been derived.

Love's mysteries in souls do grow
But yet the body is his book

John Donne
Songs and Sonnets

200 million Americans want to leave some things a mystery,
and right at the top of those things we don't want to know
is why a man falls in love with a woman and vice versa

Senator William Proxmire, 1975
Comment on National Science Foundation
grant for research into love

1

The importance
of attractiveness

The first thing that strikes us about a person is their physical appearance. Even before meeting them we are likely to have felt some degree of attraction or repulsion, and if they are of appropriate age and sex this is highly predictive of the chances of sexual and romantic involvement. In the course of being introduced, we are frequently so absorbed with the person's looks that we forget to register their names. As we get to know the person better, we may find cause to modify our initial evaluation of them. We may discover, for example, that they have qualities which partly offset their deficiencies in beauty. But however much we forgive a person for being ugly, it is very hard to forget.

The importance our society attaches to physical attractiveness is revealed in art, literature, films, advertisements and other mass media. The fairy-tale princess, the Hollywood bombshell, and the sun-tanned nature-girl who sits on the bonnet of a sports car sipping cola, are all minor variants of a cultural standard that is held before us throughout our lives. This model is difficult to describe but easy to recognise, as is its male equivalent (Prince Charming, Clark Gable, and the man who drives the sports car); its prime purpose is to define the appropriate target for romantic interest. People who fail to measure up to this standard, or even approximate to it, can hardly avoid becoming aware of the discrepancy, and the realisation can come very hard. Small wonder we are so concerned about our looks, so responsive to compliments, and take such pains to do the best we can with ourselves through exercise, diet, cosmetics and clothing.

Clinicians and counsellors see many cases in which the problem centres on concern with looks. Pathological shyness, depression and even suicide are often attributed to the patient's belief that they are too ugly to ever hope to attract a mate. Sometimes that belief is realistic, sometimes it is quite unfounded. In the condition of anorexia nervosa, a pathological thinness which afflicts mainly adolescent girls, one of the symptoms has been described as the delusion that by starving they make themselves more attractive. Few practising doctors and psychiatrists are disposed to doubt the crucial role that self-perceived attractiveness plays in our mental life.

Despite all this, there has been a great deal of resistance against conducting research on attractiveness and its ramifications. Some people have objected to the field on the grounds that it is trivial – a patently misguided criticism. Others cast aspersions on the motives of the researchers for interesting themselves in the field, implying that they must surely be perverted; this accusation may occasionally be true, but it is always irrelevant. Recently, however, the most common objection has been that the research only draws attention to a source of handicap that would be far better played down or entirely forgotten. This 'ostrich' attitude has been expressed most vehemently by women's liberationists, who of course oppose beauty contests for the same reason. While their political aims are well-intentioned, perhaps laudable, the brief of the social scientist is to study the behaviour of people as it actually is, rather than as he or anyone else would like it to be.

A considerable amount of research has now been conducted into the personal and social relevance of attractiveness. Studies have been done to assess the extent of prejudice that is operating in favour of attractive people in schools, courtrooms and other situations. The effects of attractiveness variations on life adjustment, happiness, self-concept, social attitudes and sense of humour have also been investigated. By reference to the studies that are now beginning to appear in the scientific journals, this chapter will outline the present state of evidence.

Beauty is talent
Attractive people are preferred not just for their aesthetic and sexual appeal. A popular guideline or stereotype seems to have developed in which all manner of good qualities are attributed to them. This 'halo effect' was expressed by the poet Sappho who wrote that 'what is beautiful is good', and by Schiller, who observed that 'physical beauty is the sign of an interior beauty, a spiritual and moral beauty'. Thus the hero in fairy stories and romantic novels is usually brave and charming as well as handsome, and the heroine kind and virtuous as well as beautiful. Likewise, the assumption throughout much of history and literature has been that people who are deformed in body are also likely to be deformed in mind (e.g. the fictional hunchbacks, Quasimodo and Rigoletto).

That attractive people are automatically presumed to possess other socially desirable characteristics has been demonstrated in a study by Karen Dion and associates at the Universities of Minnesota and

Wisconsin. They had a large group of men and women rate photo-graphs of people varying in attractiveness on a number of personality traits, and assess their chances of success in life. Attractive people were seen to have every advantage. They were rated as more sexually warm and responsive, sensitive, kind, interesting, strong, poised, modest, sociable and outgoing. They were also seen as likely to get more prestigious jobs, to make more competent husbands or wives and to have happier marriages. Thus, not only were they judged to be of better character and more exciting as dates; it was also assumed that they would gain more in terms of material benefits and personal happiness.

Among all these advantages there was only one exception – they were not expected to be better parents. The reason for this is not entirely clear. Perhaps it was felt that attractive parents would be more prone to having affairs and getting divorced, or more generally capitalising on their good looks by socialising in adult society to the neglect of their children. Unattractive people might be expected to find greater reward and affection in the family context and so devote themselves to their spouse and children.

Some qualities attributed to attractive people

	Attractive person	Average	Unattractive person
Socially desirable personality	65·40	62·40	56·30
Occupational status	2·25	2·02	1·70
Marital competence	1·70	0·71	0·37
Parental competence	3·54	4·55	3·91
Social and professional happiness	6·37	6·34	5·28
Total happiness	11·60	11·60	8·83
Likelihood of marriage	2·17	1·82	1·52

Students rated photographs of people varying in attractiveness; the higher the score the better. Except for parental competence, attractive people are seen to have every advantage. (from Dion and others 1972)

Prejudice in the classroom
The advantages of being attractive begin to operate at an early age. Karen Dion and Ellen Berscheid conducted a sociometric analysis of nursery school children. With this method, children are asked to name those whom they like, so the most popular child in the class can be identified as the one that is most often named. The results showed clearly that children who had been independently judged as attractive by adults were liked the most. Stereotypes relating to people's looks were detectable even in the age range 4 to 6 years. The children believed that aggressive, anti-social behaviour was more characteristic of the unattractive.

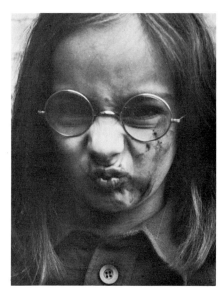

Judgement of children's behaviour is influenced by their appearance

(a) She appears to be a perfectly charming little girl, well-mannered, basically unselfish. It seems that she . . . plays well with everyone, but like anyone else, a bad day can occur. Her cruelty . . . need not be taken too seriously.

(b) I think the child could be quite bratty and would be a problem to teachers . . . she would probably try to pick a fight with other children her own age . . . she would be quite a brat at home . . . all in all, she would be a real problem.

Female students given a description of a cruel act by a 7 year old child responded according to the attractiveness of that child. For example, the above responses were obtained for (a) an attractive child, and (b) an unattractive child. (from Dion 1972)

Stereotypes favouring attractive children were also discovered in the teachers. M. M. Clifford and Elaine Walster showed four hundred teachers an identical report card, but with different photographs appended. Some teachers were given a photograph of an unattractive child and others a picture of an attractive child. Attractive children were rated by the teachers as having higher educational potential; they were assumed to have a higher IQ, parents more interested in their education, and better social relationships with their peers.

In another study by Karen Dion, the perception of delinquency was studied by giving female students a written description of a seven-year-old child's transgression at school. Attractiveness was again varied by appending a photograph to the behavioural description. The students attributed more anti-social impulses of a chronic nature to unattractive children. In general they were rated as more malevolent and likely to misbehave again in the future. In contrast, excuses were made for the transgressions of good-looking children, or else their misbehaviour was seen as an isolated incident. It seems that adults are predisposed to ascribe the trait of dishonesty to unattractive children, which means that such children may be at a distinct disadvantage when it comes to the assignment of blame for wrongdoing in the playground and the home.

Essay marks for females varying in attractiveness

	Actual quality of essay	
Appearance	Good	Poor
Attractive	67	52
Unknown	66	47
Unattractive	59	27

Students were asked to evaluate the quality of an essay supposedly written by a female co-ed. Those who were led to believe the writer was attractive gave her a higher mark — even though the same essay was used in each case. (from Landy and Sigall 1974)

Academic prejudice against unattractive people has also been found at the college level. David Landy and Harold Sigall, at the University of Rochester, had male students evaluate an essay ostensibly written by a female student. In fact, the same essay was used in each case, but with different photographs attached. The writer's ability and the quality of her work were evaluated more favourably if she was believed to be attractive, her looks being especially salient when the quality of the essay was objectively poor. It appears that beautiful people can get away with inferior work while ugly people can only avoid being discriminated against by producing consistently superior work.

This research suggests that there is a bias operating against ugly children and students in the academic setting. The bias is not only in

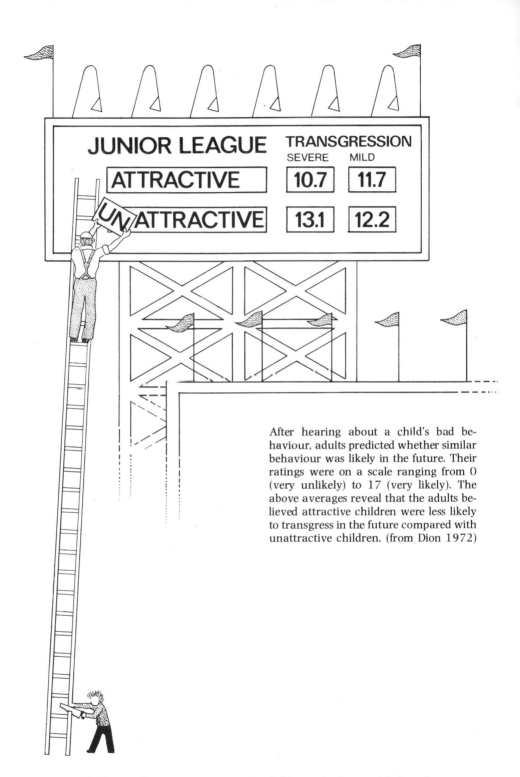

JUNIOR LEAGUE TRANSGRESSION

	SEVERE	MILD
ATTRACTIVE	10.7	11.7
UNATTRACTIVE	13.1	12.2

After hearing about a child's bad behaviour, adults predicted whether similar behaviour was likely in the future. Their ratings were on a scale ranging from 0 (very unlikely) to 17 (very likely). The above averages reveal that the adults believed attractive children were less likely to transgress in the future compared with unattractive children. (from Dion 1972)

Predicting future transgressions in children who have misbehaved

terms of expectations about the behaviour of children according to their degree of attractiveness, but also in terms of the rewards and punishments that are dispensed for equal performance. This point is important because the stereotype (i.e. expectation) could, and actually does, contain an element of truth. However, evaluating the same behaviour differently in ugly and beautiful people is a form of prejudice which cannot be justified in any way.

Consider another finding that has been reported several times: attractive female students obtain higher grade point averages than unattractive fellow students. There are three possible explanations for this. Attractive girls might actually be more intelligent than unattractive girls because beauty is an 'upwardly mobile' characteristic. There is evidence, for example, that women who marry above their social class were more attractive when young than women who marry men of the same or lower socioeconomic status (attractiveness in the studies being assessed by rating college photographs). This would mean that good looks would accumulate in the higher social classes and become correlated with intelligence. A second explanation is that teacher expectations of superior performance from attractive children would bring about a kind of 'self-fulfilling prophecy'. Within certain limits people do develop in accordance with what is expected of them. The third possible explanation is in terms of the Landy-Sigall effect. Teachers might operate direct discrimination against unattractive students, giving them lower marks for work of the same quality. Any of these processes could result in attractive students gaining better grades in college, and probably all three contribute. The 'halo effect' of attractiveness seems to have some realistic components, but others that are totally unfair and indefensible.

The scales of injustice

The finding that the classroom and playground transgressions of unattractive children are treated as more serious and less excusable than the same misbehaviours of attractive children leads to the question of whether something similar goes on in the courtroom. Are judges, juries and magistrates more likely to convict ugly offenders than beautiful ones, or sentence them more severely after conviction?

Although no direct 'field' studies have been undertaken, presumably because of practical research difficulties, suggestive evidence is available that the judicial system harbours some degree of bias in favour of attractive people. Harold Sigall and Nancy Ostrove asked students at Maryland University to read an account of a crime and then suggest an appropriate term of imprisonment for the offender. Attached to the description of the offence was a photograph of the

Average prison sentences given to female criminals

Offence	Attractive	Unattractive	Unknown appearance
Burglary	2·8 years	5·2 years	5·1 years
Swindle	5·5 years	4·4 years	4·4 years

Student 'judges' sentenced a defendant to a term of imprisonment. For burglary, a female who was unattractive, or of unknown appearance, received a heavier sentence than an attractive girl. But for a swindle – in which 'good looks' helped the crime – an attractive female received the heaviest sentence. (from Sigall and Ostrove 1975) defendant – a woman, made up to appear highly attractive for one group of students and unattractive for another. A third group of students were not given any visual portrayal of the offender.

Although the sentences suggested for the unattractive woman were no different from those dispensed to the woman of unknown appearance, the attractive woman was treated quite differently. When sentence was supposedly being passed for the crime of burglary, the attractive woman was given a much more lenient sentence than that given to the others. However, for a confidence swindle, in which she was supposed to have ingratiated herself with a middle-aged bachelor and induced him to invest in a non-existent company, a slightly stiffer sentence was prescribed for the attractive offender.

This suggests that highly attractive people who are accused of crimes that have no connection with attractiveness may be at a distinct advantage in the courtroom compared to an unattractive person accused of an identical crime. Yet if the crime is of such a nature that good looks might be instrumental (e.g. fraud) the court-room bias might react against the attractive person. Presumably animosity is incurred if the court believes that the prisoner has taken advantage of the 'God-given' gift of beauty for purposes of criminal gain.

Of course, these experiments are based on mock-court situations and we cannot be certain that similar biases occur in the real courts. We could hope for something better from qualified and experienced judges and magistrates. However, juries are by definition composed of ordinary citizens, and the more important decision (conviction or acquittal) is primarily in their hands. It seems highly probable that in borderline cases the entire decision may turn on the attractiveness, or lack of it, of the person standing in the prisoner's box.

The research to date on prejudicial processes in both the classroom and the 'courtroom' indicates that the world is generous to people who are attractive (unless they become confidence tricksters and get caught). By the same token, the world tends to be unkind in various ways to people who are unfortunate enough to have been born ugly. It might have been hoped that information about a person's actual behaviour would be sufficient to discount the effects of superficial appearance. Unfortunately for most of us, the evidence does not even offer this consolation. Looks still carry a lot of weight even when judges are provided with a concrete piece of the person's behaviour to evaluate.

Prestige value of an attractive partner
If you are not attractive yourself, it is advantageous to be associated

with someone who is. Harold Sigall and David Landy have demonstrated that observers impute positive characteristics to a man who is
romantically associated with an attractive partner.

Students were requested to give their first impression of a man
who was presented to them in one of four situations. Some saw him
accompanied by a plain woman; others by an attractive woman. (In
fact, it was the same female confederate of the experimenters whose
attractiveness was varied by changes in clothing and make-up.)
Half the subjects were led to believe that the woman was the man's
girl friend, the others were told she was unconnected with him. The
target man was rated by the subjects on a variety of attributes such
as intelligence, self-confidence, talent and likeability.

When the man was seen as escorting the good-looking girl friend,
he received the most favourable overall ratings from the observers.
The least favourable impression was given when he appeared to have
an unattractive girl friend in tow. If he was perceived as unassociated
with the girl, her looks had no influence on the impression that
he gave.

This study suggests that a man gives a better impression to other
people when he is with a beautiful woman. Presumably this is because
the observers reason that he must have some good qualities to
attract the pretty girl. If a man is seen in the presence of a plain
woman, it is apparently better that he is known to be not romantically
associated with her. Men do seem to be aware of these effects; they
are usually happy to flaunt pretty girl friends in front of their associates, but hold secret meetings with unattractive females.

Are attractive people happier?
Given all the social advantages of being attractive we might expect
that good looking people would lead happier lives than the rest of us.
Eugene Mathes and Arnold Kahn of Iowa State University undertook
a study to test this assumption.

A large group of students completed questionnaires concerning
their happiness, self-esteem and psychological health. Independent
judges assessed them for attractiveness. In the case of men, looks
had no bearing on happiness, self-pride or adjustment. For the
women, attractiveness did bear a slight but consistent relationship
with each of the three measures; beautiful women tended to be
happier, more proud of themselves, and less neurotic.

It is interesting that attractiveness should relate to happiness and
adjustment for women but not for men. This result can be accounted
for in terms of a sex difference in the value placed on physical
attractiveness. In chapter 3 evidence is presented that attractiveness
is a more highly valued commodity in women than in men, and this

would explain why it is more relevant to their happiness. Achievement and social status are more highly valued attributes in men, so we might expect to find these more closely related to their happiness and adjustment.

Attractive people tend to have happier marriages

Marriage	Men		Women	
	Good	Poor	Good	Poor
Male raters	3·7	3·5	3·7	3·6
Female raters	3·8	3·4	3·7	3·5

Young couples whose marriage was judged to be either well adjusted or poorly adjusted were rated for physical attractiveness. The well adjusted group tended to be more attractive. (from Kirkpatrick and Cotton 1951)

Marital adjustment has also been found to be associated with attractiveness. Clifford Kirkpatrick and John Cotton of Indiana University asked students to nominate instances of well-adjusted and poorly-adjusted couples amongst their friends and acquaintances. The physical appearance of these couples was then independently assessed by visiting interviewers. Results showed a preponderance of attractive people in the well-adjusted group. There was also an indication that the attractiveness of the wife was more important to the adjustment of the couple than that of the husband. Overall, the well-adjusted partners tended to be similar in degree of attractiveness, but where there was a discrepancy the wife was likely to be the better looking. This finding is consistent with the economic model of mate-selection outlined in chapter 3; women have a much harder time compensating a lack of looks with other attributes than do men.

Both these studies dealt with men and women who were in their peak years of attractiveness (around ages 20 to 30). If life adjustment is staked on physical charms to any extent, what happens when these begin to fade? Happiness, as a subjective state, is always relative to something, and no doubt one of the ways we assess our current level of happiness is by comparison to that which we have experienced in the past. Women who are attractive when young have more to lose than those who are not, and so we might predict a reversal of the beauty/happiness relationship in later life.

This possibility that attractive women may become less happy as they get older was reviewed by Ellen Berscheid and associates. The life adjustment of middle-aged people was compared with their attractiveness when young as assessed by ratings of photographs from college yearbooks. True to the above suggestion, women who were highly attractive when young as judged from their college photographs tended to be less happy and well-adjusted to their life at around the age of 50. No such relationship was found for men, again confirming the finding that physical appearance is less critical for them than it is for women.

Berscheid's finding with respect to women calls to mind the 'ageing actress syndrome' — the stereotype of the woman whose stage success was founded upon her sexual attractiveness, and who in middle-age is reduced to a pathetic, gin-soaked neurotic, waging a losing cosmetic battle against encroaching wrinkles, greyness, and other signs of old age. Perhaps the interest of the men in her life had also been contingent on her beauty, and had subsequently evaporated. Apparently, an inability to grow old gracefully is a danger faced by many attractive women. If happiness is an ultimate criterion, plain women may come into their own in the autumn of their lives.

Attractiveness, attitudes and fantasies

We have seen that a person's awareness of whether or not they are good-looking is relevant to their self-concept and happiness at different stages of their life. What other aspects of mental life might be measurably influenced by variations in attractiveness?

The question of whether attractiveness would be reflected in social attitudes and reactions to different kinds of sexual humour was investigated by Glenn Wilson and Tony Brazendale at the Institute of Psychiatry, London. A group of ninety-seven female student teachers aged between 18 and 21 was given an attitude questionnaire covering a wide range of controversial topics and also asked to rate their enjoyment of each of a series of forty-two seaside postcards. (These postcards, which depict risqué jokes in cartoon form, are something of an institution around the coastal resorts of Britain.) The physical attractiveness of the students was rated by lecturers from a different college who did not know any of them personally.

Results showed a tendency for the unattractive girls to be more religious, puritanical, idealistic and opposed to sexual freedom. Their favourite postcards were ones which depicted sexually attractive girls being discussed, propositioned, molested or otherwise approached by eligible men. Apparently, plain girls try to protect themselves against awareness of their disadvantage in the permissive society by adopting puritan attitudes to rationalise their lack of sexual involvement. At the same time, they enjoy fantasies concerning male advances, identifying with the shapely, much sought-after girls in the postcards and thus vicariously obtaining some of the male attention of which they are deprived in real life. The male equivalent of this kind of wishful thinking might be the weedy, inadequate little man who becomes a devoted James Bond fan.

Attractive girls tended actively to dislike the 'male chauvinist'

a   b

Looks are related to humour preferences

'Female-passive' cartoons such as (a) are enjoyed by unattractive girls, presumably because they are able to identify in fantasy with the girl who is receiving the male attention of which they are deprived.

Attractive girls liked 'female-offensive' cartoons such as (b). Perhaps this is because they have the confidence and experience to contemplate a more active and dominant sex role. They tended to dislike jokes in which the female was portrayed as the victim of male lechery, perhaps because they are tired of being the target of crude male advances in real life.

jokes, perhaps because they have had their fill of lecherous male attention in the course of their everyday life. Instead, they favoured jokes that featured passive male victims and dominant females threatening sexual initiative, e.g. derision of the man's genitalia or sexual performance (female chauvinist jokes?).

Whatever the precise interpretation of these findings, they do indicate that a girl's attractiveness or unattractiveness to the opposite sex have effects upon her mental life which are detectable through the media of attitudes and humour. No doubt similar dynamics could be observed with male subjects, though they would probably be less marked because physical appearance is a less salient feature in the lives of men.

Beauty, then, is more than skin deep. The extent to which we possess or lack it is important in a number of life's central areas. It affects our chances of attracting a mate, of obtaining a job, completing an academic qualification, and perhaps even receiving an acquittal on a criminal charge. It affects the way other people evaluate us, our confidence, happiness and other mental processes. All this seems good justification for studying it, apart from the fact that it is intrinsically a fascinating topic.

In the following chapters we look at the question of what constitutes attractiveness, the elements that are most important in determining it, the chemical basis of attraction and its evolutionary development, how all these elements differ from person to person and between cultures. We also consider the conditions under which people are prone to falling in love and their choice of a person with whom to do it.

2

What is attractive?

As we have said, attractiveness is easier to recognise than to describe. Philosophers, artists, writers, and everyone else, have argued throughout the centuries as to the definition of beauty, but arrived at few useful conclusions. Many argue that analysis of attractiveness into components, such as hair colour and distance between the eyes, is fruitless because it is the overall impression or 'gestalt' that counts. Others are dazzled by the bewildering variety of tastes that occur between individuals and between cultures, and end up by doubting that any general rules can be established. Again, others point out that there are various different forms of attractiveness (aesthetic beauty, sexual desirability, and so on) and our evaluation depends on what we have in mind – whether we are looking for a fashion model, a partner, a playmate, or what? There is truth in all these reservations, but still we are not prevented from extracting useful generalisations.

This chapter attempts to define and analyse attractiveness as far as the evidence so far permits. In doing so, we focus on the visual, physical characteristics that determine initial sexual interest, i.e., the things that 'turn us on' and the things that make us sexually attractive to others. These are important preliminaries in the processes of mate selection and falling in love, but do not constitute the full story; additional factors relating to these areas are discussed in the two following chapters. For the moment we are concerned with the fundamentals of immediate physical appeal.

Agreement on who is attractive

The fact that there are still ongoing debates as to who and what should be described as attractive has not impeded social scientists very much in their investigation of the topic. This is because scientists use 'operational' definitions of their concepts, i.e., they define variables in terms of the techniques used to measure them. In the research of the authors, a five-point scale is given to the judges along with some instructions on how to use it. This is shown below:

Scale of sexual attractiveness (physical)

1	2	3	4	5
Not at all attractive	Slightly attractive	Moderately attractive	Very attractive	Extremely attractive

Instructions to raters

1 Please use the scale above to indicate to what extent you think each person would be *attractive, on average, to most members of the opposite sex.* Try to disregard any peculiar preferences of your own and anything you may know about the personality of the individuals you are rating. Try to ignore also the way in which they are dressed or presented at the moment, i.e. rate them only on 'native' attractiveness

2 Try to use each of the five categories about equally, or at least make some attempt to distribute your ratings across the scale

3 The data will remain absolutely confidential and will be used only for group research in which the names of subjects are discarded before final analysis

When a standard rating scale such as this is used there is a good deal of agreement between different raters as to how attractive various people are. In a typical study demonstrating this consensus, Anthony Kopera and colleagues at Northeast Illinois University presented eighty-four slides of women to a large group of students and asked them to rate them on attractiveness. Analysis of the results revealed that each slide was given remarkably similar ratings by the different judges. Even comparing male and female judges, almost perfect agreement was found in the ratings of attractiveness.

The extent of agreement was expressed in terms of a correlation coefficient. These coefficients range from 1 where there is perfect agreement, through zero where there is no agreement whatsoever, to −1 where there is a perfect inverse relationship. The correlation between the ratings of the male and female subjects in this particular study was 0·93, which means that there was an extremely high degree of concordance between the sexes in their attractiveness ratings.

So the sex of the rater does not effect the rating of feminine beauty to any extent; nor does age, occupational status, or geographical region. In a study by A. H. Iliffe of University College of North Staffordshire, twelve photographs of women's faces were ranked for 'prettiness' by more than four thousand readers of a national daily newspaper. According to Iliffe the photographs represented a narrow range of attractiveness levels; none was included which could be called either 'very beautiful' or 'plain'. Despite this, great uniformity in the rank orders produced by different individuals was found. It did not seem to matter whether the rating was done by men or women, young people or old people, professionals or unskilled workers,

Welshmen, Scotsmen or Londoners. The correlations were all between about 0·80 and 0·95.

This finding of high inter-rater correlations with respect to attractiveness is very important for two reasons. It tells us that our measurement scale is reliable, and therefore probably doing its job well. It also tells us something about the concept of attractiveness; it reassures us that although there is some variation in tastes, beauty is by no means entirely in the eye of the beholder. Any individual differences in taste that are observed appear within a context of very good general agreement.

The concordance of attractiveness ratings is not always as high as those reported above. Exceptionally high reliability coefficients are usually only found when ratings are based on photographs. As soon as more information about the ratees is introduced into the experimental situation the extent of agreement is reduced. Thus if the judges are allowed to view the subjects live, or interview them (as they do in beauty contests), the interjudge correlation tends to be lower. This is because a greater variety of characteristics such as the way they walk, talk, sniff, blink and smile becomes available to the rater, and different raters concentrate on different things. It follows that there is greater agreement among strangers as to who is attractive than among friends who know the subjects well. When the raters know the ratees they are likely to base their judgements on personality characteristics as well as sheer physical attractiveness and the instructions to disregard these aspects in the rating scale shown above are poor protection against this tendency.

How accurately do we perceive ourselves?
To what extent do we see ourselves as others see us? Do we have much insight into our own level of attractiveness? There is some correspondence between an individual's self-perception and the opinion of external judges but it is much lower than the agreement amongst different outside judges. Bernard Murstein of Connecticut College, for example, found correlations of 0·33 for men and 0·24 for women. This represents a positive but fairly low agreement between subjective (self) ratings and objective (other person) ratings of attractiveness.

The most obvious explanation of this lack of agreement between one's view of oneself and the opinion of others is in terms of the cue-confusion effect just described. Probably nobody knows the ratee better than himself, and insofar as he has information about himself that is not available to the casual observer his judgements are bound to differ. Note that from the point of view of researching native, sexual attractiveness, it is the objective rating that is more valid than the subjective one, despite the fact that the latter is based upon more information. For present purposes, the additional information is irrelevant and only confuses the issue.

Individual differences in conceit and modesty probably represent another source of error. No doubt some people habitually over-rate themselves and others are inclined to be self-effacing. The possible extent of interference due to modesty was illustrated in a study by Norman Cavior of West Virginia University. He found that three-quarters of a group of school girls had ranked themselves as the least physically attractive person in their class! Although it is not clear whether the girls were really being serious, Cavior concluded that many girls become so obsessed with their imperfections that they are unable to view them relative to the deficiencies of others.

What men look for in women
As a general rule, sexual attraction is based on the differences between the sexes. It follows that the points of maximum difference will be the most attractive and arousing; the more exaggerated these differences, within reason, the more sexually attractive they will be. Basically, the idea of beauty treatment and make-up is to do just this — to emphasise some of the ways in which the female face is different from that of a male (fuller lips, narrower eye-brows, softer complexion, absence of facial hair). Large breasts are usually seen as attractive up to the point where they lose firmness and begin to droop downwards; this is associated with ageing and is therefore less attractive. The narrow waist and relatively broad hips of the human female are also major sexual stimuli. Most of these signals have a biological basis (see chapter 9) but others are apparently socially conditioned. For example, we regard long hair and fingernails as sexy and feminine even though, without cutting, those of a man would grow just as long.

In attempting to define what constitutes an ideally attractive female we are aided by the fascinating spectacle of the beauty show. Following a series of local and national finals, every year one girl is eventually crowned 'Miss World', and we might expect her characteristics to give us a good clue as to what men look for in women. A recent averaging of winners of this contest over the years revealed an English-speaking model, aged 21 years, 5 ft 8 ins in height, blonde with brown eyes, and measuring 35–24–35. Of course, some of these specifications are more invariant or telling than others; for example, the age and measurements do not change a great deal from year to year but language and colouring do.

From the point of view of the research psychologist the Miss World Contest does not provide an ideal definition of the perfect female. The girls are judged neither by experts, nor by a representative sample of men; instead they are assessed by a peculiar assortment of show-business personalities. No properly constructed rating scales are used and the results are not put to any statistical tests. Not surprisingly, the result is often markedly counter to popular opinion, such as that expressed by bookmakers' odds. In addition, there are certain controls on entry; mothers, married girls and film stars are usually excluded, and many highly attractive girls regard it as beneath themselves to enter. Many factors other than physical attractiveness also enter into the judgement, e.g. the way the girls respond to a somewhat banal interview, the clothes they wear, and the political issues arising from the fact that a country is being chosen as well as an individual. Despite all this, the girls that are chosen are undeniably very attractive.

Another model for female sexual attractiveness is the 'playmate' that appears in men's magazines such as *Playboy* and *Penthouse*. Typical vital statistics for this kind of girl are 37–24–35, i.e. slightly larger breasts than Miss World, but waist and hips about the same. Their average height is somewhat less than Miss World, presumably because they do not depend upon making an impression on a remote stage.

Compare these statistics with two groups of women who are not distinguished by any large measure of sexual attractiveness. One is the clothing model who appears in women's magazines such as *Vogue*. She tends to be narrower all the way down, but especially at the breasts and waist, so that the hour-glass effect is reduced somewhat. A rather extreme example is Twiggy, with a 31–24–33 figure. Another comparison is with the average British woman, who has a figure of about 37–28–39. Of course she is older than the others, and tends to be larger all over, particularly at the waist and hips.

These comparisons confirm that sexual attractiveness in women is magnified by large breasts and hips set against a narrow waist, i.e., exaggeration of the way in which the average female form diverges from that of the male. It is important that these fleshy protruberances are not flabby or sagging, which means that the ideal woman must be fairly young (late teens or early twenties). Older women may, of course, attempt to delay or disguise their loss of shapeliness with uplift bras, corsets, etc., but there is obviously a limit to this.

Individual preferences

We can probably accept Miss World and the 'playmates' as representing a fair average of the kind of girls that men find most attractive. We have also established that this is a worthwhile exercise since there is some consensus among men about who is attractive. But within this context of agreement there are also some measurable group and individual differences in preferences.

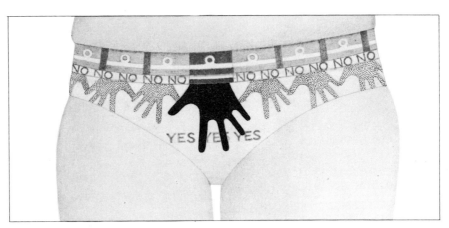

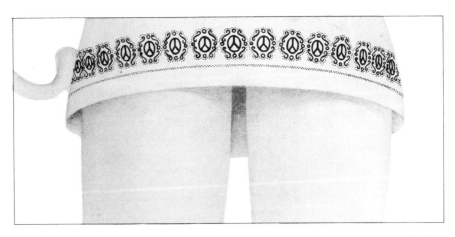

Characteristics of men who like various female body types (see table overleaf)

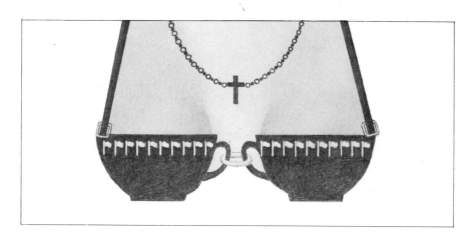

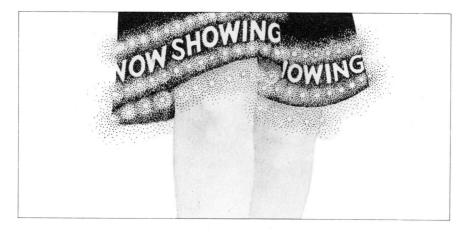

Andrew Mathews and colleagues at Warneford Hospital, Oxford, showed men a set of pictures of women culled from various sources ranging from 'soft' pornography to women's fashion magazines. Some of the women in the pictures were fully clothed, some completely naked, and others partially dressed in bikinis or underwear. In line with previous studies there was a fair amount of accord as to which women were most sexually desirable. The most desirable women were described as attractive, sexually inviting, graceful, young and slender. Adjectives applied to the less desirable women were: 'vulgar', 'available', 'prostitutes', 'old', and 'gross'.

The following individual differences were also observed: Introverts preferred their women more fully dressed and thinner than extraverts. Apparently introverts are likely to feel overwhelmed by nude and well-developed women and feel more at ease with thin and thoughtful looking girls. A group of homosexual men liked women that could be summarised as non-threatening — those described as sexless, unavailable, fully dressed, respectable, prim and antiseptic. Finally, social class differences were also apparent. Manual workers preferred conventional, well-dressed women rather than those who were 'trendy'. When the question was reframed so that the men were asked which of the women they would favour as long-term mates, their preferences shifted towards women who were elegant and conventionally well-dressed, while sexy and provocative poses were less valued than before.

There is a popular belief that men can be classified into three groups — breast men, buttocks men, and leg men — depending on the region of female anatomy most salient in determining their likes and dislikes. Jerry Wiggins and his colleagues at the University of Illinois

Part of anatomy	Size	
	Large	Small
Breasts	Readers of *Playboy*	Non-drinkers
	Smokers	Religious
	Sportsmen	Depressed
	Frequent daters	Submissive
Bottom	Obsessional	Persevering
	Passive	Non-sporting
	Guilt-prone	
	Need for order	
Legs	Non-drinkers	Extravert
	Submissive	Exhibitionist
	Self-abasing	Nurturant
	Socially inhibited	Sociable
Overall figure	Ambitious	Persevering
	Drinkers	Introvert
		Upper class

Men can be classified according to their preferences in female shapes. (from Wiggins and others 1968)

asked a group of students to rate nude female silhouettes that varied in the three body parts, and complete a questionnaire to assess their personality. The results confirmed the general expectation that men can be reliably classified according to the part of the female anatomy that most preoccupies them.

There were also some interesting relationships with personality. Men who liked big breasted women tended to be readers of *Playboy*, smokers, sportsmen, and frequent daters; they were extravert and masculine in their tastes. By contrast, men who preferred small breasts tended to drink very little, to hold fundamentalist religious beliefs, and to be mildly depressed and submissive. Men who liked big buttocks were characterised by a need for order, obsessionality, passiveness and a sense of guilt; men who liked small buttocks were persevering in their work and uninterested in sport. Men who liked large legs tended to abstain from alcohol, were submissive and self-abasing, and inhibited in social situations; men who preferred small legs were extravert and exhibitionistic. Preference for a large figure overall was linked with a high need for achievement and a high consumption of alcohol; those who liked small figures were per-severing and introverted.

This evidence hardly justifies an excursion into personality dynamics as it stands, but it does suggest that the preferences of men for different types of female figure are linked with their general personality and life style. The finding of a sporty, extravert, playboy-type man who likes women with large breasts is both intuitively appealing and consistent with the Mathews study. So is the finding of a submissive, abstinent, religious, introvert type of man who feels more comfortable with women whose breasts are small in proportion to the rest of their bodies and thus register as less flagrant sex symbols.

One other rather amusing study of personality in relation to sexual preferences was conducted by Alvin Scodel at the University of Ohio. He tested Freud's theory that men with 'oral' personalities – defined as having a strong need for dependency – would prefer women with large breasts. The results were statistically significant but in the opposite direction; dependent men actually tended to prefer small breasts. Thus Freud's notion that a liking for big breasts stems from oral frustration in childhood has yet to be empirically supported.

What attracts women?

The features of women that are attractive to men are fairly widely recognised, but there is more of a mystery concerning the physical characteristics of men that are sexually attractive to women. As we have said in chapter 1, women are less concerned about physical attractiveness in men, or at least, their basis of judgement is more complex and variable. Contrary to the belief of many a male, they are seldom interested in the circumference of his flexed biceps, the size of his penis, or whether or not he is circumcised.

In a recent poll conducted by a New York newspaper, *Village Voice*, 100 men were asked which parts of their body they thought would 'turn on' women the most. Then a group of 100 women were polled using the same question concerning the male features that were superficially most attractive. Both groups protested that it was somewhat irregular to view males as sex objects at all, but when pressed for specific responses, the results were very different for the two sexes. Men thought that women would most admire a muscular chest, shoulders and arms, and a large penis, as suggested by tight trousers. The women, however, claimed to be 'disgusted' by these; instead, they frequently cited small buttocks as the attribute they most admired in men. No less than 39 per cent of the women nominated this region as the most attractive part of a man. Other attractive features in men, according to women, are tallness, slimness (especially a flat stomach) and various expressions in the eyes.

Another study of female preferences among male physiques was conducted by Paul Lavrakas at the Loyola University of Chicago. On the basis of depth interviews with a large group of women he decided that the most significant body proportions were those involving the arms, legs, upper trunk and lower trunk. Therefore he drew up a set of male silhouettes which differed in the relative sizes of these areas, and asked seventy women between the ages of 18 and 30 to rate them as paired comparisons.

The favourite male physique emerging from this procedure had thin legs, a medium–thin lower trunk and a medium–wide upper trunk – leading to a kind of V-look. The 'pear-shaped' look, with either a thin upper trunk or a wide lower trunk, was the least popular. A number of personality differences were also found. Clean-living, extravert, sporty women liked muscular men, while neurotic, radical drug-users tended to prefer thinner, more linear figures. Traditional, relatively mature women preferred broader figures overall than younger 'liberated' women.

Many of the idiosyncratic preferences could be accounted for by saying that the women liked figures that tended towards similarity with their own or with that of the most important man in their life at the time. Thus women who were overweight themselves, or who were in love with an overweight man, opted for relatively broad figures, and vice versa. This might explain why smokers and drug-users like thinner men – they probably tend to be thinner themselves.

What men imagine women admire (%) **What women really admire** (%)

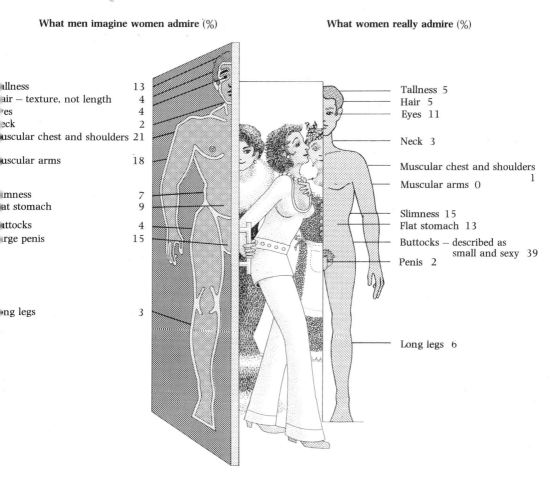

...llness	13
...air – texture, not length	4
...es	4
...eck	2
...uscular chest and shoulders	21
...uscular arms	18
...mness	7
...at stomach	9
...ttocks	4
...rge penis	15
...ng legs	3

Tallness 5
Hair 5
Eyes 11

Neck 3

Muscular chest and shoulders 1
Muscular arms 0

Slimness 15
Flat stomach 13
Buttocks – described as small and sexy 39
Penis 2

Long legs 6

The fallacy of what women look for in men

Both men and women were asked to nominate that part of the male anatomy most admired by females. The results demonstrated that what men imagine women admire and what they really do are almost opposites! (from *Village Voice* survey)

Height and a man's attractiveness

Tallness is often cited as attractive in men, and a word of elaboration is called for because its connection is complex. Firstly, it is a cardinal rule of dating and mating that the man be taller than the woman, so *relative* height may be just as important as absolute height. It is possible, for example, that a man appeals most to a woman when he is an optimal degree taller than her – say five or six inches taller.

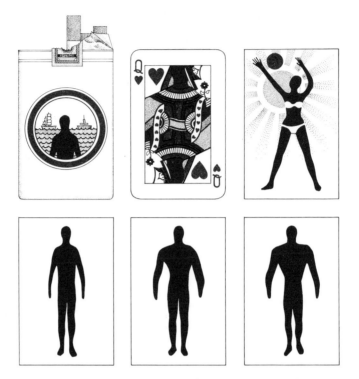

Individual differences in women's preferences among male physiques

Characteristics of women preferring each of the above silhouettes:

1   Nervous, concerned with appearance, heavy smoker
2   Thin, cigarette smoker, non-drinker, card-player, sportswoman
3   Young, extravert, non-smoker, non-drinker

A much greater discrepancy than this and the woman is likely to feel that her own looks are not enhanced or that as a couple they appear ridiculous.

Superimposed on the relative height factor, however, is an absolute height factor that is very probably mediated by social status. A connection between perceived height and status was demonstrated in a study by Paul Wilson at Australian National University. A man was introduced to different students as either a student, demonstrator, lecturer, senior lecturer, or professor. Later the students were asked to estimate his height. As he climbed the academic status ladder, he gained two and a half inches in the eyes of the students.

This finding has been cross-checked in various ways. In a survey conducted by the *Wall Street Journal* of careers followed by graduates from the University of Pittsburg, it was found that men over 6 ft 2 ins

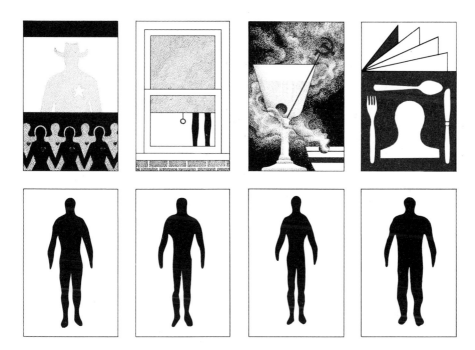

4 Conventional, card-player, film-goer, non-sportswoman
5 Older, experienced, liberated, living with a man
6 Rebellious, drinker, drug-user
7 Mature, overweight, tolerant, conservative, reads a lot
   (from Lavrakas 1975)

in height had salaries $12\frac{1}{2}$ per cent higher than those of men under six feet. In another study, 140 recruiters were asked to make a hypothetical hiring choice for a sales job between two equally qualified applicants, one 6 ft 1 in tall and the other 5 ft. 72 per cent expressed a preference for the tall man compared with only 1 per cent for the short one (27 per cent would not express a preference). Also relevant is the fact that every American president elected since at least 1900 has been the taller of the two major candidates.

Since height is clearly associated with social status in men, and social position is an important determinant of overall male attractiveness, we might expect some association between tallness and male attractiveness. This is what surveys such as that conducted by *Village Voice* do actually show.

Health, vivaciousness and arousal

Another determinant of what is attractive (for men and women) is apparent healthiness. People who are constantly complaining of ill health are seldom perceived as sexy, however much they may evoke a maternal or protective response. The evolutionary significance of this preference for healthy mates is obvious. Probably this is the basis of the stress we place on clear skin as a component of beauty — skin tone is an excellent indicator of a person's state of health. We are also attracted to people who show a general zest for life; drive, creativity, curiosity and sexual interest are all related 'life forces', important in determining sexual attractiveness.

That arousal or vivaciousness is attractive is well illustrated in a study by Eckhard Hess of the University of Chicago. He asked men to rate the attractiveness of two photographs of the same girl, identical in every respect except that in one picture her pupils had been touched us so as to enlarge them. Most men chose the one with the larger pupils as more attractive, even though they were frequently unable to spot the difference between the two photographs. It is known that our pupils dilate when we are highly aroused and interested in what we are looking at, and it seems that this may be transmitted as a sexual signal without our awareness. Another well-known instance of a sign of arousal being seen as attractive is the value we place on the maidenly blush; not only does this signify modesty but also sexual awareness.

Men prefer a girl who emits arousal signals

These two photographs are identical except that in one case the pupils have been retouched so as to make them larger. Arousal as indicated by pupil size is itself arousing — most men find the girl on the left more attractive, even though they may be unable to spot the difference between the two pictures.

Facial features

Intuition suggests that facial features are also important in determining attractiveness. Unfortunately, little is known about the
relevant aspects except that symmetry and an absence of blemishes
make for attractiveness. This point was rather ingeniously demonstrated by Sir Francis Galton in the last century, using the technique
of composite portraiture which he pioneered. A large number of faces
are superimposed onto a photographic plate by fractional exposures
to produce a single face which averages the features of all the different
people. In particular, the features which are common to most of the
faces are retained, while blemishes and peculiarities are eliminated.

> The result is a very striking face, thoroughly ideal and artistic, and
> singularly beautiful. It is indeed most notable how beautiful all
> composites are. Individual peculiarities are all irregularities, and
> the composite is always regular.
>
> (*Inquiries into Human Faculty*, 1883)

Galton's finding implies that all that is required of a beautiful face
is an absence of extremes. The nose should not be too long, or too
short; the eyes should not be too close together or too far apart, and
so on. Add to this a smooth, unblemished complexion, which we have
said is a sign of good health, and we have a face that will probably
be judged beautiful. Contrast this with the kind of physique that is
created by the averaging process, e.g. the vital statistics of the average
British woman. Bodies have to be exceptional, but apparently faces
are better not.

Of course, the averaging of faces was done for men and women
separately, so that we have at least two average faces – one male and
one female. True to our principle that the opposite sex is attractive
because it is different, we might predict that slight exaggeration of
the points of difference might enhance attractiveness. We suggested
that women use make-up to highlight the way in which their face
differs from that of a man. Probably a woman who is naturally very
feminine in her facial features would also tend towards prettiness –
large eyes, narrow eyebrows, soft complexion. Similarly, a man with
a rugged, masculine face (strong jaw, bushy eyebrows, leathery skin)
is probably more likely to be described as handsome. On the other
hand, the degree of difference between the sexes has definite evolutionary limits upon it (see chapter 9), so great extremes of divergence
cease to be attractive.

Cultural differences in what is judged as attractive

To some extent, our judgments of physical attractiveness are
influenced by cultural standards of beauty. Anthropologists claim

that there is no universal agreement as to what constitutes attractiveness. The most celebrated examples of cultural variation are the Arab preference for plump women, and a liking for drooping or 'pendulous' breasts in certain primitive tribes. These exceptional cases, however, should not blind us to the existence of valid generalisations. They should be viewed rather as extremes of the variation which is always present, whether between different cultures, or between different individuals in the same culture.

Explanations for these variations may be found in other characteristics with which the attribute is associated; for example, in our culture we value a suntan partly because it indicates that one has been skiing or on a tropical holiday and it imparts prestige. In other cultures, plumpness may be valued because of its associations with sumptuous living (therefore wealth) or maternity, and drooping breasts because they suggest age-related status. Women successful in the 'Miss World' competition or selected to adorn the pages of *Playboy* magazine probably represent the human norm for desirability; other things being equal they would be desirable to all men.

It is noteworthy that although standards of beauty do vary slightly from one society to another, there is fairly universal agreement that the physical appearance of women is more central to their overall attractiveness than it is for men. Three explanations have been offered for this. One, possibly lighthearted, suggestion draws attention to the preponderance of male anthropologists operating in the field. A second theory is that the differential value placed on attractiveness is secondary to a sex differential in power and decision-making. According to this theory, social inequality has resulted in physical appearance becoming one of the few bases on which to choose one woman against another. It would predict that Women's Liberation might eventually succeed in eliminating this relative emphasis on women's looks as political and economic power is redistributed between the sexes. A third possibility, which is described in more detail in chapter 9, is that of a biological basis to the difference. A study of the evolution of primate sex invitations suggests that men respond instinctively to visual signals emitted by women in a manner that could not be reversed by social changes. No doubt this debate will be with us for some time to come.

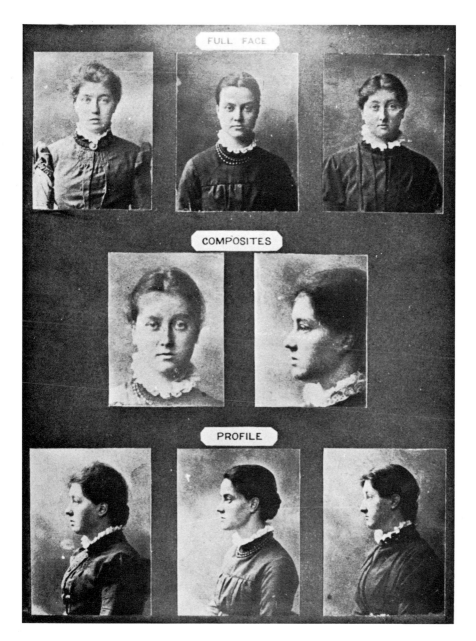

Composite portraits

The Victorian genius Sir Francis Galton developed a technique for superimposing photographs of people's faces so that their features are averaged. The result is a single face that often appears beautiful because it is devoid of blemishes and peculiarities.

3

Choosing a partner

It is often said that a man takes more care in selecting a car than he does in choosing a mate. This is almost certainly not true, though he frequently ends up better suited by his car than by his wife. The reason is that with cars there is a relatively small number of fairly obvious criteria on which to base a decision, e.g. reliability, speed, and comfort. In choosing a partner, a far greater number of criteria have to be taken into account and the information relating to them is usually only received by slow instalments as part of the process of getting to know the individual candidates and the range that is available. Marriage bureaux and computer-dating agencies offer only a minimum degree of help in the selection process by arranging an introduction to someone who is available, and roughly similar in age, education and interests.

In this chapter we outline the research concerned with the question of how human couples arrive at their partnership, i.e. the physical and psychological attributes that are important in determining the pairings. We shall also consider whether it is possible to predict the long-term prospects of these relationships once they are established.

The economic model of mate selection
Although it may seem cold-blooded and unromantic to appraise a potential partner in terms of commodity values, this is what actually takes place at an emotional or subconscious level. Each of us has a list of implicit criteria or attributes that we regard as important in a mate, e.g. looks, intelligence, social status, wealth, sense of humour, temperament, availability. A prospective partner is assessed on each of these attributes and the resulting ratings are weighted according to the importance that we attach to the different attributes. The weighted attribute ratings are then added to arrive at a single 'eligibility score' for that candidate. This process occurs unconsciously and often almost instantaneously. Although it may seem

Attribute	Importance weighting (0–5)		Rating (0–5) of prospective mate A	Rating (0–5) of prospective mate B		Product A	Product B
Looks	5		0	5		0	25
Intelligence	3		5	1		15	3
Wealth	3	**×**	3	0	**=**	9	0
Sense of humour	2		1	5		2	10
Availability	1		2	4		2	4
Religion	1		3	2		3	2
Eligibility score						**31**	**44**

How we choose between two prospective partners

Above is a much simplified example of economic mate selection. The person making the choice has a number of selection criteria to which he or she attaches varying degrees of importance. Each 'candidate' is rated on the criterial attributes; these ratings are then multiplied by their importance and the products summed to give an overall eligibility score. In the example above, the good-looking, amusing and available prospect B is preferred to the intelligent and relatively wealthy A. The list of criteria and the importance assigned to them vary according to the sex and personality of the selector and the nature of the relationship envisaged (e.g. casual sex or marriage).

complicated, it is typical of the kind of calculation that our brains are making within a split second thousands of times a day.

The list of attributes used in mate selection and the relative importance of them varies from person to person. It also varies according to the precise purpose for which a partner is being selected, e.g. whether for casual sex, an impressive arm-decoration, or marriage. Nevertheless, there are some general rules that can be adduced and research has revealed some of the most important factors that are operative in determining who ends up with who.

The priority of physical appearance
When people are asked to say what qualities they regard as most important in a partner, virtues such as character, honesty, sincerity, and warmth are often cited. Physical attractiveness is usually mentioned but relegated to a position of lesser importance. There is an impressive body of research evidence, however, which indicates that

physical good looks are of overwhelming importance in determining partner preferences. Indeed, in actual practice the other factors may hardly enter the picture at all.

The pre-eminence of physical appearance is most striking in studies dealing with the formation of first impressions. A blind date provides an ideal opportunity of studying how two people take to each other; therefore a series of experiments have been carried out using the 'computer dance' situation. In this method students are given a ticket for a dance on the understanding that they accept a partner for the evening who is chosen for them by the organisers. Later their opinions of their partners are assessed in various ways, such as by asking them how much they liked their partner and whether they intend to pursue the relationship any further. The first thing these studies revealed was a very close association between the physical attractiveness of a partner and the extent to which they were liked.

Elaine Walster and associates at the University of Wisconsin checked this finding by independently rating the students for attractiveness. This safeguard was necessary just in case the students in the earlier studies had rated their partners as attractive merely on account of liking them. Walster had the students rated for attractiveness while they were obtaining their tickets at the box office. Later they were also assessed for personality, intelligence and social skill — variables which we might think would be important in making a good impression on a date. The students were paired on a random basis with the one restriction that the man was always taller than the woman. Questionnaires were given at intermission to find out how much the partners liked each other, whether they wanted to see each other again, and so forth. A clear finding emerged that the more physically attractive the date, the more he or she was liked. The other attributes such as personality and intelligence were of no consequence; physical attractiveness, pure and simple, was all that mattered, and this applied equally for men and women.

The importance of attractiveness may not seem surprising when we consider the reactions generated by those who show romantic affection for a distinctly unattractive person. Such people are subject to quizzical glances and even interrogated about their reason for involvement. What does seem surprising, though, is the overwhelming importance of appearance in determining how much the students liked their dates. One would have thought that personality, intelligence and social skill would have played some part.

Of course the other attributes might count for a lot more if the period of enforced partnership was made longer, so that people would have more time in which to get to know each other. Against this, however, must be put the possibility that in the real-life situation potential partners might be rejected on the basis of their looks even before allowing a test period of a couple of hours such as in the 'computer dance' experiment. Physical appearance is the first thing we notice about a person, and the looks criterion might have to be passed before any of the other attributes are considered at all.

Looks and the fear of rejection

The computer dance situation is artificial in that it does not arouse any strong fear of rejection. Though a partner to whom one has been assigned may not wish to pursue the relationship any further, they are at least obliged to be polite and cooperative for the duration of the evening. In real life, people of lesser desirability might well feel that they are likely to be rebuffed if they are too ambitious, and so they might only seriously consider dating people who are also unattractive.

This 'level of aspiration' question was investigated by Ellen Berscheid and associates at the University of Minnesota. They designed an experimental situation in which subjects were required actively to choose a dating partner. This was achieved by showing them a set of photographs of members of the opposite sex and asking them which one they would like to meet. Results showed that the subjects, especially the females, tended to be realistic in that they chose to meet partners of a similar level of attractiveness to themselves. Fear of failure appeared to act as a moderating influence on their choices.

It seems that while both men and women prefer a highly attractive partner, they are prepared to settle for less if necessary. A person's ambitions in the love stakes depend on their own level of physical attractiveness, such that they are only likely to do anything about obtaining a partner if they feel that there is a real chance of being accepted.

Similarity of attractiveness in established mates

Since people only aspire to partnerships with others who are not too far removed from themselves in terms of physical attractiveness we would expect that real-life dating and married couples would show similarity on this attribute.

Irwin Silverman of the University of Florida sent his students out to observe courting couples in such places as bars and theatre lobbies where they could be watched unobtrusively. Attractiveness was rated on a five-point scale, with male observers rating the women and the female observers independently assessing the man in each couple. An extraordinary degree of similarity in attractiveness between the dating partners was found. For 85 per cent of couples, they were not separated by more than one scale point. Silverman also hypothesised that couples who were similar in attractiveness would be happier with each other and would therefore engage in a greater amount of physical intimacy (holding hands, walking arm-in-arm, and so on). The data revealed that 60 per cent of couples who were highly similar in attractiveness level engaged in some kind of intimate contact, compared to 46 per cent of moderately similar couples and only 22 per cent of those lowest in similarity.

In another rather ingenious research design, a selection of wedding photographs were obtained and cut apart so as to separate the married couples. The individual portraits were then randomised and rated by a group of judges who did not know how they had been originally paired. This revealed a close correspondence between the attractiveness of the partners; the people in the photographs had chosen a partner of very similar level of attractiveness to themselves. Studies of this kind have confirmed that looks are a very important consideration in choice of dating and marriage partners as well as in assessing a blind date.

The association in these studies is never perfect, though, and this suggests that other factors apart from looks are also instrumental in mate selection. Where there is a notable discrepancy in looks between a couple, our economic model would imply that the less attractive individual offers compensation on some other attribute such as social status, wealth or physical skill. The reader will recall the well-known anecdote about the actress who proposed marriage to Bernard Shaw, pointing out how marvellous it would be if their progeny combined her looks with his brain. Although on this occasion Shaw was motivated to present the alternative possibility, trade-offs of this kind are sometimes made in practice.

Looks count more for women

The commodity value of physical attractiveness is higher for women than for men. Men are better able to compensate for unattractiveness with other qualities such as social position and sense of humour. This statement is based upon massive evidence but we may illustrate by reference to two types of study.

One approach to the question has been quite simply to ask men and women to rate the importance they assign to various attributes in the opposite sex. These studies consistently show that men are more concerned about the looks of women than vice versa. In a recent study by Richard Centers of the University of California, Los Angeles, both male and female students were asked to list qualities that were especially desirable for each sex. The attributes considered to be most desirable for females were physical attractiveness, erotic ability, affectional ability, and social ability. Characteristically male attributes

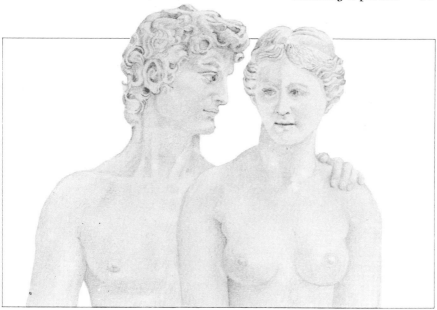

Desirable attributes in a partner

	Males	Females
1	Achievement	Physical attractiveness
2	Leadership	Erotic ability
3	Occupational ability	Affectional ability
4	Economic ability	Social ability
5	Entertaining ability	Domestic ability
6	Intellectual ability	Sartorial ability
7	Observational ability	Interpersonal understanding
8	Common sense	Art appreciation
9	Athletic ability	Moral–spiritual understanding
10	Theoretical ability	Art–creative ability

People were asked to rate the qualities they thought were important in partners of either sex, but particularly so for (a) males and (b) females. The above table gives the qualities in order of importance. (from Centers 1972)

were achievement, leadership, and occupational and economic ability.

To find out whether the attractiveness factor is, in practice, more strongly weighted by men than women, other researchers have correlated looks with popularity as measured by frequency of dating. Here the results show that physical appearance is a much stronger predictor of dating popularity for women than it is for men. For example, Berscheid and colleagues found that the number of dates that a person had in the last year was correlated 0·61 with attractiveness ratings for females, but only 0·25 for males. Of course, the males tend to take more initiative in arranging dates, but they still have to get accepted, and it is interesting to discover that their looks count for little in this respect.

The point about male initiative raises the question of whether the greater importance assigned to looks in women than men is socially conditioned or of biological origin. With the recent revival in women's consciousness we may find that some sex differences such as this will retreat slightly. On the other hand, the principles of primate evolution (chapter 9) suggest a biological interpretation; we appear to have evolved in such a way that males respond to female invitation signals presented visually. The social code no doubt acts to reinforce the greater visual responsiveness of males, but is insufficient to account for its origins.

The age differential in partner choice

Although we tend to choose partners of approximately the same age as ourselves, the man is on average about three years older than his female partner. It is commonly believed that this age differential results from earlier female maturation. This may possibly apply in the case of teenage couples, but for older people a different explanation is necessary and this is readily provided by the differing market values for attractiveness and achievement in men and women respectively.

In women attractiveness is of primary importance and this is rapidly lost with age. Achievement, on the other hand, tends to increase with age. The desirability or market value of a man therefore tends to continue or increase for some time beyond the teenage years, while that of a woman declines. In other words, the loss of looks with age in a man is more readily compensated by social status and other attributes than it is for a woman.

Male attractiveness: dominance or competence?

Generalising from the observation of primate colonies we might think it is male dominance that is most sought after by women. Commonsense, however, might lead us to think that simple dominance is not sufficient – a woman usually likes to think that a man is skilful and knowledgeable before he starts to tell her what to do.

John Touhey of Florida Atlantic University set up an experiment to evaluate the relative contributions of physical dominance and competence to female perception of male attractiveness. Eighty students were paired off for the purpose of performing a maze task. The males were required to guide their female partner either verbally or physically while she attempted to find her way through the maze. The couples were then told whether they had scored above or below average. Later, the females were asked to rate their partner on such items as 'desire to date'. The ratings indicated that the males who had been physically dominant and competent were liked most. However, males who had been physically dominant but incompetent in the assistance they had rendered were liked the least.

The moral is clear. It is no use a man adopting cave-man tactics with a female prospect if he is also ham-fisted. If women enjoy being pushed around at all, it is only by a man who knows what he is doing. It is unfortunate that Touhey did not repeat his experiment reversing the roles of the men and women in the task, so that we could see how men react to being dominated by competent and incompetent women.

Women are attracted to dominant men only if they are competent

	Physical	Verbal guidance
Competent males	12·1	10·5
Incompetent males	7·2	8·0

Men were instructed to help a female partner in a maze task using either physical or verbal guidance. Later the women were asked to rate how much they were attracted to their male partner. Physically dominant men were most liked if they were competent, but least liked if they were incompetent. (from Touhey 1974)

Love and the Oedipus complex

Before leaving the area of physical appearance in relation to partner choice there is a psychoanalytic theory that might be noted. Sigmund Freud believed that in choosing a partner we are seeking a substitute for our opposite-sex parent. Thus a man should be attracted to women who resemble his mother in some way, while a woman ought to like men who remind her of her father. Freud argued that this occurs unconsciously and stems from the Oedipus complex (the tendency for little boys to desire their mother sexually while jealously hating their father) and its female equivalent, the Electra complex. In a theoretical paper on the nature of love, Australian psychiatrist G. L. Christie states (with characteristic psychoanalytic omniscience): 'We know that unconscious Oedipal yearnings can cause a man to fall in love with a woman who resembles his mother, sister or daughter.' He offers no evidence to support this claim, but illustrates it by relating how Charles Dickens became involved in an affair with a young woman following the marriage of his daughter of the same age, and soon after the death of his mother.

There is no real evidence to support Freud's theory, but a study by Alan Miller of California State University, Los Angeles, is interesting in connection with it. Miller had a group of women rank a series of photographs of male physiques from those that looked 'most like their father' to those that looked 'least like their father', with several inter- mediate scale positions being available. Later they were asked to choose the physique that they would most desire in a lover. Results showed a statistically significant tendency for them to choose in a lover a physique that was either most or least like their father. While hardly constituting proof of the Freudian notion, this study does suggest that attitudes towards the opposite sex parent may influence one's choice of a mate.

Attitude similarity

Although attractiveness appears to be of overwhelming importance in determining initial desirability ratings, and continues to exert a major influence on the judgements of women by men well past the stage of early acquaintance, certain other factors begin to enter the picture as more information is gained about the prospective mate. One such factor that has been the subject of several research studies is the extent to which the social and political attitudes of the two people correspond.

People like attractive partners and those with similar attitudes

	Similar attitudes	Dissimilar attitudes
Attractive male	12·0	10·6
Attractive female	12·7	11·3
Unattractive male	10·4	9·9
Unattractive female	11·0	9·5

Students on a 'blind date' were given a partner with similar or dissimilar attitudes to themselves. After the date they indicated how much they liked their partner. The highest ratings were given to attractive partners and those who held similar attitudes. (from Byrne and others 1970)

There is evidence that we prefer people who hold attitudes similar to our own. Don Byrne and associates at Purdue University asked students to evaluate a fictional person on the basis of his answers to a questionnaire covering a wide variety of social issues. These answers were made similar or dissimilar to the subject's own (predetermined) attitudes. Also, to each questionnaire was attached a photograph of either an attractive or unattractive person. The subjects clearly preferred attractive people and those who were represented as having attitudes similar to their own.

The trouble with this study is that no information other than attractiveness and attitudes was made available to the subjects, so it is not surprising that these attributes determined the preference ratings. To cover this criticism Byrne conducted another experiment in which students were paired off for a blind date according to their actual responses to an attitude and personality questionnaire. Half the students were paired with someone similar to themselves in attitudes and personality and half were paired with someone completely dissimilar. Physical attractiveness ratings of the students were also made. When the subjects were interviewed after their date, it was found that both attractive people and people with similar personality and attitude scores were found to be most desirable. Both similarity and attractiveness were also related to the physical proximity of the two individuals while they were talking to the experimenter after the date — attractive and compatible couples tended to stand closer together. In a follow-up at the end of the academic term, similarity and attractiveness both predicted accurate memory of the partner's name, whether they had seen each other since the blind date, and their desire to date that person in the future.

This study constitutes good evidence for attitude similarity as a factor entering into partner preferences. At first sight it appears to be incompatible with the Walster study that showed physical appearance as the only important variable. However, Walster and colleagues did not assess the couples for similarity on personality or any of the other dimensions that they measured — instead they focused on different degrees of presumed desirability. In this way they missed making a very significant discovery, that as regards personality and attitudes the people we find most desirable are people just like ourselves. One's own personality and attitudes are best almost by definition.

Computer dating studies might well underestimate the importance of attitudes in determining partner preferences. Generally they permit very little opportunity for an exchange of ideas. In the computer dance situation, for example, the couple may never get around to discussing their religious and political philosophies. In contrast, attractiveness is omnipresent. In real life there is a gradual unfolding of attitudes, so their relative influence probably increases for some time as the relationship develops and the partners gain progressively more information about each other. A recent finding that attitude similarity is more important in determining choice of marriage partner than dating preferences is consistent with this idea.

The 'gain phenomenon'

Another factor that influences our feelings about another person is whether or not they seem to like us. As a general rule we like people who appear to like us, but it is important that they do not come across as insincere or ingratiating. Elliot Aronson and Darwyn Linder compared the effects of being consistently nice to people with being

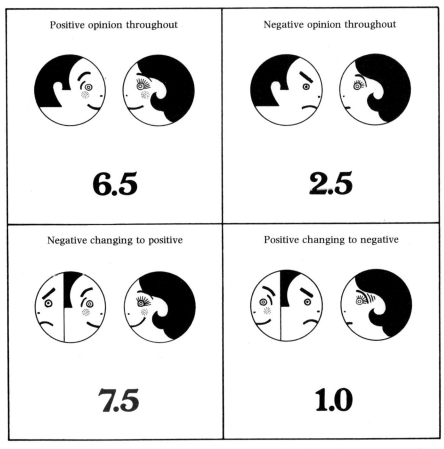

Positive opinion throughout	Negative opinion throughout
6.5	**2.5**
Negative changing to positive	Positive changing to negative
7.5	**1.0**

Ratings of attraction to a 'stooge' whose opinions of the subject were varied systematically

People most like others who progress from making negative statements about them to positive. (from Aronson and Linder 1965)

N.B. Scores indicate how much the subject liked the 'stooge'

consistently nasty, and with changing from one attitude to the other. They got students to converse with a confederate over a number of meetings. The confederate then made remarks about the subject to the experimenter which subjects were permitted to 'accidentally' overhear. Later the students were asked to rate their degree of liking for the confederate on the basis of their conversations with him. Not surprisingly, they liked a confederate who had made uniformly complimentary remarks about them, and disliked those whose comments were persistently derogatory. But best of all, they liked those whose comments had progressed from unfavourable to favourable during the course of the experiment.

This study suggests that the best way to win new friends (and lovers) is to start by appearing to dislike them, without being too insulting, and then to show progressive interest and approval. There are various possible interpretations of this 'gain phenomenon'. One is that early reserve and disdain reduces the chances that the later warmth will be perceived as habitual or ingratiating. A related explanation links the effect with the success of the tactic of playing hard to get. A resistant girl is likely to generate more passion in the end than a constantly rewarding girl because the high value she places on her own affection is accepted by others including her suitor.

Self-esteem is a negotiable asset

Another interpretation of the gain phenomenon is in terms of self-esteem. Several experimental studies have shown that low self-esteem persons are less demanding in their expectations of other people, including opposite sex partners. Elaine Walster, for example, showed that women whose self-esteem had been lowered experimentally were more attracted to an attractive young man than women whose self-esteem had been raised. Other studies have shown that men who are low in self-esteem are less likely to attempt to date a physically attractive woman than men who are high in self-esteem. If it is supposed that appearing rude or indifferent to somebody on first acquaintance has the effect of lowering their self-esteem, even temporarily, then we might expect them to be rendered more vulnerable to whatever charm we are later able to produce. This is unlikely to be a total explanation of the gain phenomenon, but it might well be a contributing factor in some circumstances.

People with high self-esteem are able to attract mates who are closer to their ideal than people with low self-esteem. Bernard Murstein of Connecticut College had ninety-nine engaged couples fill out a personality questionnaire in four different ways: (1) for themselves as they really were, (2) for themselves as they would ideally like to be, (3) for their fiancé(e) as they believed he or she to actually be, and (4) for an ideal spouse. The measure of self-esteem was taken as the discrepancy between a subject's real self and his ideal self. The results showed that people with low self-esteem as indicated by this self-ideal discrepancy had settled for partners who had fallen shorter of the requirements for their ideal spouse than people of high self-esteem. In order words, people who think highly of themselves (whether or not they have any justification for doing so) seem able to attract a partner with whom they are more satisfied than people who have a low opinion of themselves. In passing, it is interesting to note that nearly all of the individuals concerned were deceiving themselves in regarding their partner as a closer approximation to their ideal than really was the case according to the partner's report on his or her own personality.

Personality: similarity or complementation?
With respect to personality factors in mate selection, two opposing theories have had widespread popularity. One theory is that we gravitate towards someone similar to ourselves (like marries like); the other is that we choose or fall in love with someone who complements us in some way (opposites attract). We have seen that similarity theory is vindicated as regards attitudes, self-esteem and physical attractiveness. It also applies to demographic variables such as age, race, religion and social class, even if part of this effect is mediated by geographical proximity (a high proportion of people marry somebody who grew up in the same neighbourhood as themselves).

The complementation theory finds its most obvious support in connection with sex (gender); most people fall in love with a member of the opposite sex. There are also a number of temperamental and personality characteristics for which complementation might be thought to apply. For example, we would expect a person who is dominant in social situations and likes to do a lot of talking to find himself drawn to a quiet, submissive mate. What does the evidence show?

A study by David Nias suggests that neither similarity or complementation has much application in the area of personality. He administered a lengthy personality questionnaire to 650 married couples in the English Midlands. For only one question out of a hundred did the couples show any tendency towards being opposite. This item concerned reading; if one partner liked reading the other tended to dislike it. Most of the other items showed a slight tendency towards concordance but not sufficient to say that similarity theory was really supported. Several other studies of this kind support a similar conclusion; there is a very slight resemblance in personality between married couples but to all intents and purposes they may be said to marry at random in this respect.

Ronald Sindberg and associates in Wisconsin enlisted the aid of a computer matching bureau in a rather novel approach to the question of personality factors in mate selection. They compared a group of

Factors conducive to marriage

A comparison of couples who got married after a computer introduction with couples who did not shows that compatibility is based on similarity of personality and interests rather than complementation. (from Sinberg and others 1972)

Factor	Type of difference
Interest in sport	Large difference in either direction, less often married
Height	Large difference in either direction, less often married
Interest in fine art and music	Man higher than woman, less often married
Need for affection	Man higher than woman, less often married
Concrete–abstract	Couple congruent, more often married, man more abstract, less often married
Submissiveness–dominance	Large difference in either direction, less often married
Sober–happy-go-lucky	Couple congruent, more often married
Confident–apprehensive	Couple congruent, more often married
Undisciplined–controlled	Large difference in either direction, less often married
Relaxed–tense	Man much more tense, less often married
Witty–placid	Couple complementary, more often married

twenty-five couples who had got married following a computer intro-duction with previous, unproductive pairings involving the same fifty individuals. For all of the pairings, whether they had led to marriage or not, the computer had matched couples in terms of similarity in age, race, education, religion, social class, and several attitude and personality traits. This leaves us with a very sensitive test for the effects of the personality and other factors on which pre-matching had not occurred.

Several factors emerged on which congruence between the couple increased the chances of them getting married. The couple were more likely to marry if they were of similar height, had a similar degree of interest in sport, and were similar in concreteness of ideas, serious-mindedness, confidence, control, and dominance. It was not conducive to marriage for the man to be more interested in fine arts and music than the woman, or for him to be more tense or have a higher need for affection. Complementation applied on only one dimension, described as 'witty versus placid'. Apparently there is only room for one wit in a marriage relationship. It is notable that the complementation principle did not apply to dominance versus submission, for this is one trait that is frequently cited by exponents of the theory as one for which it should operate. In fact, the reverse was found in this study.

Overall, then, similarity theory comes out with more support than complementation theory in predicting partnerships on the basis of personality, but even the effect of similarity is very slight and requires refined techniques to magnify it before it becomes detectable.

Predicting marital success

We have presented some evidence as to how people form partnerships, how they are likely to respond to a new acquaintance and what sort of person they are likely to marry. It would be nice to report on research showing what sort of couple will enjoy a successful marriage. Unfortunately it is not really possible to do this because no satisfactory evidence is yet to hand. The reason is that the two criteria of marital success that have been employed in the research, reported happiness and stability, are both very faulty.

In a typical study using the index of self-reported happiness, Lewis Terman found a slight tendency for 126 'happily married' couples to be less alike in personality than 215 'less happily married' couples. The correlations (0.11 and 0.20 respectively) were, nevertheless, still both in the positive direction, meaning that even the happily married couples were more alike than different.

Apart from the fact that this is a very weak result, there is a problem in distinguishing the happiness of marriage from the happiness of the individuals that comprise it. We know that people who come from happy homes tend to make happy marriages, but probably they bring their happiness with them to the relationship rather than derive it from the marriage. In other words, people who are in-dividually happy are also likely to be happy in marriage, but this does not mean that the marriage has necessarily added to their level of happiness. For all we know, the marriage may have subtracted more from their prior happiness than a person who entered the state in a miserable condition. This kind of problem has usually been over-looked in assessing marital success.

The other index of marital success, stability, is equally vexed. We know that Catholic and Jewish marriages end in divorce less often than non-religious and mixed-religion marriages. We know that people who are geographically and socially mobile have a higher divorce rate than people who are stationary in these respects. But does this mean that the marriages that survive in the low risk groups are more happy than those that survive in the high risk groups (or even those that were disbanded)? Certainly not; we have no way of knowing how the divorce rate of a group relates to average marital happiness.

If we are to be able to make any worthwhile statements about the factors conducive to successful marriage we first need to find some more satisfactory criteria of success. At the moment we are better placed to tell people what they are probably going to do than whether or not they ought to go ahead and do it.

4

Falling in love

Nearly all of us at one time or another in our lives experience an emotional upheaval that we describe as being in love. Probably this is the most dramatic and mysterious experience ever to befall us, and most people have an insatiable curiosity about it. It may produce great euphoria or the deepest hurt, which makes it unique among our emotions. The preoccupation of Western society with love is evident in poetry, drama, novels and other forms of art and entertainment. But despite the assertions of some anthropologists, the phenomenon is neither of recent origin nor restricted to our culture. Although not always thought of as a necessary prelude to marriage, romantic and passionate love has appeared at all times and places.

Poets, dramatists, philosophers, psychoanalysts and others have provided us with a wealth of insights into what it feels like to fall in love – its delights, its pains, its vicissitudes, characteristic sequences, and so forth. What can the scientist possibly add to help to clarify the picture? The answer is that psychological science sets out to define the various aspects of love more precisely – usually quantitatively – and specify the conditions under which they are most likely to occur. Like most forms of social behaviour, love is so complicated that almost anything folk wisdom has to say about it is bound to be correct – in some circumstances. Even directly contradictory assertions are both likely to be true; the problem is to find out when each of them may be expected to apply.

For example, it is sometimes true that absence makes the heart grow fonder and sometimes true that a lover is out of sight, out of mind. How could the contradiction between these two statements be resolved? One scientific hypothesis that has received indirect experimental support was put forward by the British psychologist Hans Eysenck. He suggested that rapid recovery from the loss of a loved one is typical of extraverted persons (people who are active, sociable and impulsive), while perseveration and pining are characteristic of introverts (quiet, thoughtful, controlled people). No doubt many other

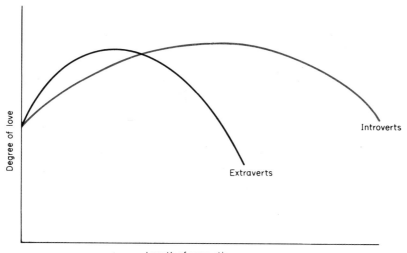

'Absence makes the heart grow fonder' or 'Out of sight, out of mind'?
Introverted people, suggests H. J. Eysenck, take longer to get over broken or
geographically disrupted romances than do extraverts. Therefore, both the above
proverbs may be true, but for different personality types.

variables are also important in determining which of the above
proverbs are applicable at any one time; the research needed to
identify them has yet to be done. But this is the manner in which
science may contribute to an understanding of complex phenomena —
by painstakingly testing different theories to see if and when they
apply.

A second question that is sometimes raised is whether we want to
know anyway. The comment of Senator Proxmire quoted at the front
of this book is typical of the kind of resistance that is sometimes put
up against investigating deeply personal and emotional topics. These
misgivings stem from the fear that self-conscious awareness of a very
human experience such as love will in some way detract from its
value and enjoyment. Yet historically such fears have always proved
unfounded. Galileo did not destroy the 'story of a starry night', nor
have the insights of Darwin undermined our appreciation of a pea-
cock's tail display. If anything, the beauty and wonder of these things
is enhanced by our increased understanding of them — an entirely
new sympathy with nature may be generated. In addition, there are
many professional workers such as psychotherapists and marriage
guidance counsellors who might profit from factual knowledge in the
area of love; the opponents of research appear to forget that many
people suffer great pain and unhappiness in these areas which is
unlikely to be alleviated by the promotion of continued ignorance.

Loving versus liking

The first problem that must be faced in attempting a scientific analysis of love is defining the phenomenon we are concerned with. This has proved a particularly difficult task since many different experiences and emotions have been implicated by different writers and theorists. For example, emotions as far removed as joy and despair have often been cited as indicating that a state of love exists. Two approaches have been taken to the problem of definition — separating love from other conditions such as liking and infatuation with which it may be confused, and identifying different kinds of love. We begin with the former.

Harvard psychologist Zick Rubin has constructed a questionnaire that separates loving from liking. The two scales were constructed according to the way in which various kinds of attitudes towards another person cluster together. The liking scale includes statements which imply that the target person is admirable, respectable, and similar to oneself; loving involves a need to be with the person, a predisposition to help them even at great expense to oneself, and a desire to be intimately and exclusively absorbed.

Rubin's two scales were completed by 182 dating couples at the University of Michigan, first with respect to their current boy/girl friend, then with respect to a close friend of the same sex as themselves.

Examples of items from Rubin's scales

Liking
Favourable evaluation
I think that John/Mary is unusually well-adjusted
It seems to me that it is very easy for John/Mary to gain admiration
Respect and confidence
I have great confidence in John/Mary's good judgement
I would vote for John/Mary in a class or group election
Perceived similarity
I think that John/Mary and I are quite similar to each other
When I am with John/Mary, we are almost always in the same mood

Loving
Attachment
If I could never be with John/Mary, I would feel miserable
It would be hard for me to get along without John/Mary
Caring
If John/Mary were feeling badly, my first duty would be to cheer him/her up
I would do almost anything for John/Mary
Intimacy
I feel that I can confide in John/Mary about virtually everything
When I am with John/Mary, I spend a good deal of time just looking at him/her

With items such as the above it was possible to differentiate loving from liking.
(from Rubin 1970)

A fair degree of separation was found between the loving and liking scales in the sense that endorsing one set of items did not necessarily imply endorsement of the others. Liking and loving were more closely associated for men than for women (correlations of 0·56 and 0·36 respectively), which supports the notion that women discriminate more sharply between the two sentiments. As a consequence, it ought to be more possible for a woman to fall in love with a man that she dislikes than for a man to love a woman he does not like.

Love scores of men (for their women) and women (for their men) were almost identical, suggesting that the two sexes experience love to a similar degree. However, women tended to love their same-sex friend more than men loved their same-sex friend. This ties in with the idea that a man who cares intimately for another man is a 'sissy', whereas women are naturally more affectionate regardless of sex. The liking scores also revealed a difference between the sexes. Notwithstanding their greater separation of loving from liking, women tended to like their partner more than their men liked them. Perhaps

Average love and liking scores for dating partners and same-sex friends

	Women	Men
Love for partner	91	90
Liking for partner	89	85
Love for friend	65	54
Liking for friend	80	78

Scores on Rubin's two scales suggest that women tend to like their partners more than men do. Women are also more likely than men to feel love for their same-sex friend. (from Rubin 1973)

a man needs to feel some romantic inclination towards a woman before taking her out, whereas a woman may go out with a man on the basis of liking alone. We shall see later that women do tend to be more practical with respect to matters of the heart than do men.

One interesting check that Rubin ran on the validity of his scales was to observe the amount of eye-contact engaged in by the couples as they waited in a room prior to an experiment. Couples who loved each other a lot, according to their scores on the love scale, were found to spend more time looking into each other's eyes. This impression of the oblivious lovers all wrapped up in each other calls to mind the song lyric 'I only have eyes for you'. Enjoyment of eye contact as an end in itself seems to be characteristic of loving rather than liking.

Love versus infatuation
Many people like to maintain a distinction between love and infatuation. Love is believed to be mature, lasting, sensible and altruistic, while infatuation is described as childish, capricious, irrational and

selfish. Unfortunately, this distinction cannot be confirmed easily by empirical methods because it is evaluative rather than substantive. In other words, relationships are described as loving when they are seen as good and virtuous, and called infatuation when one is motivated to dismiss them as inappropriate and undesirable. Thus, other people's romantic experiences are more likely to be seen as infatuations than one's own, and our own current involvement is likely to be viewed as true love while earlier defunct relationships are (retrospectively) dismissed as infatuations.

Realistic versus romantic love

A related but non-evaluative distinction is that between realistic and romantic love. Since it has been possible to separate these two types of love by the questionnaire method, some research has been conducted into their occurrence. American sociologist D. H. Knox found that married people tended to have a more realistic conception of love than single people. It seems that experience with the institution of marriage tends to make people more realistic about the nature of love. This was especially so in the case of women — they were less likely than men to retain a romantic view of love with marriage.

Knox also found that people whose parents were divorced or dead tended to have a more romantic view of love than those with parents still living together. This is an interesting finding, but the explanation for it is not clear. Perhaps observing the quarrels of one's parents is a good way of averting an overly idealistic view of man–woman relationships. Alternatively, from a more positive perspective, it may be that the absence of parental ties and expectations gives greater freedom to seek romantic attachments. Or again, people without the emotional support of their parents may have a greater need for intimate involvement with another person such as might be found in a romantic love affair.

Styles of loving

A rather more comprehensive typology of love has been produced by John Lee of the University of Toronto. Analysis of a long questionnaire covering all aspects of a person's relationship — how it began, how soon intimacy occurred, whether jealousy was strongly felt, the effects of separation, the nature and frequency of arguments, break-ups and reunions, and so forth — revealed three primary types of loving that were fairly independent of each other. These were described as *Eros* (characterised by immediate physical attraction, sensuality, self-confidence, fascination with beauty, close intimacy and rapport with the partner), *Ludus* (love that is playful, hedonistic and free of commitment), and *Storge* (which is affectionate, com-

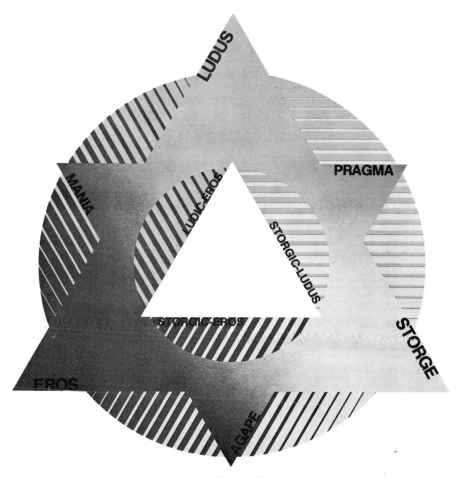

A typology of love

John Lee has identified three fairly independent 'primary' types of love: *Eros* (love of beauty), *Ludus* (playful love) and *Storge* (companionate love). Between these are various blends and mixtures, including *Mania* (obsessive love), *Pragma* (realistic love) and *Agape* (altruistic love). The further apart on the diagram the more incompatible these approaches to love are likely to be. (from Lee 1975)

panionate and devoid of passion). Three blends of these primaries were also identified: *Mania* (feverish, obsessive and jealous love), *Pragma* (practical, realistic, and compatibility seeking) and *Agape* (altruistic, patient, and dutiful).

According to Lee, the relationships amongst these different types of love can be represented geometrically as in the diagram below. The distance between any two types of love indicates the discrepancy or degree of incompatibility between them. If the two parties to a relationship have a widely disparate approach to love, misunderstanding is inevitable. For example, a ludic lover may resent a storgic partner for trying to trap him into a relationship, while she accuses him of playing games just to get her body. Eros insists on rapid intimacy, while storge may be enhanced by postponing sex. And so on. Two storgic lovers would be expected to have the best chance of a lasting relationship, while two ludic lovers would have the least chance. However, the ludic lovers might have a lot more fun while it lasts – after all, this is what they seek. It is presumed that most people enjoy some variety of different kinds of loving but have a general preference for one above the others.

When Lee administered his questionnaire to samples of English and Canadian lovers a few demographic differences emerged. Canadians were slightly more likely than English to try to cool off the partner's passion. Women were more likely than men to describe their lovers as holding back their emotions. Younger respondents tended to be more manic than older ones. Working-class men reported more sexual difficulties than professional men but there were no education or class differences with respect to the major types of love. Lee has since verified his typology with samples of older people (up to the age of 65) and on a group of homosexual males; the same variety of attitudes towards love was observed.

Whether or not Lee's classification proves to be the ultimate, it is clear that the concept of love is not unitary. No wonder so many adolescents ask the question 'How do I know when I am in love?' No wonder also that the best answer which can usually be offered is 'You'll recognise it when it comes along'. There are many different kinds of love, some of them fairly unrelated, and this must be kept in mind in evaluating the research which follows.

Who falls in love and when?

Girls tend to start having romantic experiences at a younger age than boys, and up until the age of about 20 they also have more of them. However, consistent with the findings of Knox, women become relatively realistic about falling in love when marriage is contracted or imminent. From this stage onwards, it is men who report a greater number of love experiences.

William Kephart, a Philadelphia sociologist, obtained responses to a questionnaire about experiences of love and infatuation from over a thousand male and female college students aged 18 to 24. The typical age of first infatuations was 13 and the first experience of love typically occurred at 17 – in each case about six months later for boys. The girls reported a greater number of infatuations than the boys and were slightly more likely to have experienced love. After the age of 20, the cumulative number of romantic experiences reported by males continued to increase, while that for females actually declined. Kephart interpreted this as meaning that as a woman approaches matrimony her previous loves are rejected because they impinge on the monogamistic ideal. This implies a greater measure of rational control over romantic inclinations in adult females than males. Contrary to popular belief, women seem to be less vulnerable and compulsive in the matter of love than men. In Lee's terms, they favour Pragma and Storge while men incline towards Eros and Mania.

Romantic experiences reported by American college students

	Girls	Boys
Median times infatuated	5·6	4·5
Median times in love	1·3	1·2
Median age at first infatuation	13·0	13·6
Median age first time in love	17·1	17·6

Girls tend to have romantic experiences at a younger age than boys, and more of them in their teens. After the age of 20, and especially after marriage, men report more romantic experiences than women. (from Kephart 1967)

This suggestion that women may be cooler in matters of romance than men is supported by several different findings. We have seen that women are less influenced by physical appearance than men. When social class lines are crossed, they are less likely to marry down than men. In Kephart's study, the percentage of those reporting that they were very easily attracted to the opposite sex was nearly twice as high for males as females. It is perhaps also relevant that twice as many men reported having loved an older woman (61 per cent) as women reported having loved a younger man. What is more, the females who had been romantically involved with a younger man showed evidence of maladjustment on a personality inventory and relatively poor college grades, which was not the case with males who had been involved with older women.

Finally, the difference in romantic orientation between men and women is seen in their answers to the question: 'If a boy (girl) had all the other qualities you desired, would you marry this person if you were not in love with him (her)?' Nearly two-thirds of boys said 'no', but less than one third of girls did so. Apart from placing less value on physical attractiveness, women apparently also regard love as less important in marital choice than men do. The reply of one girl was illuminating: 'If a boy had all the other qualities I desired, and I was not in love with him — well, I think I could talk myself into falling in love!' This is an exceptionally clear statement of pragmatism.

Certain personality variables have also been connected with proneness to the experience of love. One such variable is that described as 'internal–external control'. 'Internals' are highly autonomous people who feel that they can influence the course of their lives themselves, by skill and good judgement. 'Externals' feel themselves to be victims of forces beyond their control – luck, fate, and suchlike. Kenneth and Karen Dion of the University of Toronto compared these two types of people on a questionnaire relating to various aspects of romantic experience.

As predicted, 'internally controlled' people were less likely to report having been in love than the 'externals', and when they did feel romantic attraction it was viewed as less mysterious and volatile. The internals were also more strongly opposed to an idealistic view of romantic love than externals. Compared to males, the females were more likely to have experienced romantic attraction, but, again, more realistic and practical in their orientation towards it. For example, women were more likely than men to concede that a person can fall in love more than once and with more than one person at a time.

Claims of being in love have also been shown to tie in with a person's total life situation. Sociologist Evelyn Duvall had more than three thousand adolescents fill out a questionnaire which asked whether they were currently in love and collected a great deal of other information about social background and future plans. Teenagers claiming to be in love at the time (25 per cent of the boys and 36 per cent of the girls) appeared to be actively repudiating their parents' values in certain ways. They were inclined to disparage the kind of marriage their parents had, but were planning to drop out of college relatively early in favour of early marriage themselves. Duvall interprets her findings as suggesting that adolescent love may reflect a teenagers' search for identity, and is therefore more likely to occur in young people with low self-concepts who look to marriage as an escape from an unpromising life situation. Teenagers who find a satisfying sense of identity within their own families, and in their vocational aspirations, are 'less urgent about cutting loose from their parents and developing adolescent love affairs'.

The Romeo and Juliet effect
We have seen that adolescents who are rebelliously disposed towards their parents are more likely to report being in love than those who place a higher value on their family and home life. What happens to a budding relationship if the parents of one or other of the parties express opposition or attempt to interfere with it in some way? There is some evidence that parental opposition to a relationship may paradoxically result in a strengthening of the love bond in a young couple.

In a study of dating and married couples in Boulder, Colorado, Richard Driscoll and colleagues found that couples who perceived a high degree of 'parental interference' produced higher love scale scores. Furthermore, a follow-up some months later revealed that where parental interference had increased, so had the couple's passion as registered on the love scales. Similarly, Rubin found higher love scores in couples with different religions compared to couples who shared the same religion, although this finding applied only to couples who had been together for less than eighteen months (recall the higher divorce rate of mixed-religion couples).

There is evidence, then, that under certain conditions, barriers that might otherwise prevent or destroy a relationship can, at least temporarily, act to fertilise the blooming of romantic love within it. One way of explaining this effect is in terms of what is called the 'cognitive dissonance' theory of attitude change. The 'logic' or dynamics may be expressed as follows: 'Everything is against us and yet we are still together, therefore we must be very much in love.' Social isolation might also serve to heighten the experience of love in couples who do not have parental consent. It is natural that young people who fall into conflict with their family for any reason will seek solidarity within an alternative social unit (in this case their courtship or marriage).

We should not forget the possibility that some weaker relationships are actually disbanded in response to parental pressure, leaving only the deeper, more intense relationships to remain. This would also make for a correlation between parental opposition and love scores in the relationships which survive. Nevertheless, parents who seek to interfere with an 'unsuitable' love match are warned that it could boomerang on them if they are unsuccessful in breaking up the relationship.

Playing hard to get
Not all the opposition to a relationship comes from outside. Sometimes the primary obstacle to a person's love is reticence on the part of the desired partner. Could this barrier also act to heighten the sensation of love? Folklore has it that a lover who plays hard to get is in the end appreciated more by the pursuer.

Some experiments have been carried out to see if men and women who are perceived as hard-to-get become more attractive to their suitors. For example, Elaine Walster and co-workers had computer dates telephone a girl with whom they had supposedly been matched in order to arrange a meeting. Actually, it was always the same girl on the end of the telephone – a confederate of the experimenter. For half of the men she played easy to get, being delighted to receive his call and grateful to be asked out; for the others she accepted a coffee date with some reluctance because she had many other dates and was

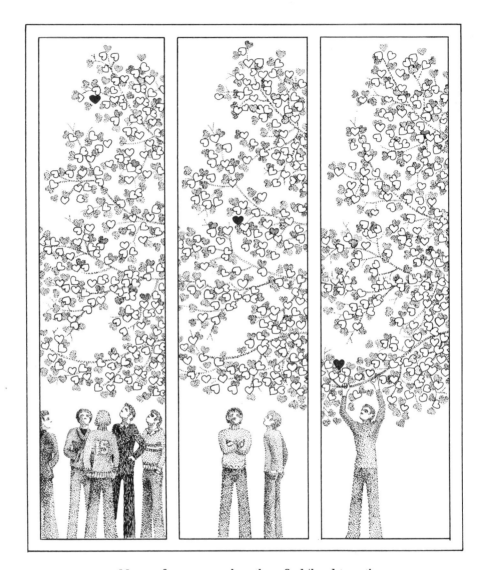

Men prefer women who others find 'hard to get'

	Selectively hard to get	Uniformly hard to get	Uniformly easy to get	No information
Number of men choosing to date each woman	42	6	5	9
Rating of how much they expected to like each date	9·4	7·9	8·5	8·6

Men given a choice of 'computer dates' tended to prefer those who had expressed interest in themselves but not other men. (from Walster and others 1973) not sure that she wanted to get involved with anyone new. After this conversation, the man's first impression of his date was assessed. The results of this and many other similar experiments failed to support the hard-to-get hypothesis. The girls seemed to be equally desirable under the two conditions of attainability.

Faced with a great deal of evidence that hard-to-get dates do not inspire more passion than those who are easily obtained, Walster and associates decided to revise their hypothesis. Perhaps the most desirable date is one who is apparently very keen on you (i.e. easy for *you* to get) but hard for anyone else to get. An experiment was devised to test this 'selective difficulty' hypothesis. In a computer date design rather like the above, one girl appeared *generally easy to get*, making it clear that she was keen to date anybody the computer assigned her. Another girl made it clear that she was *generally hard to get*, i.e. not particularly eager to date any of the men assigned to her. A third girl was *selective*, i.e. eager to date the subject but not interested in any of his rivals. Two other potential dates were *control* girls who gave no information concerning their preferences. This time the hypothesis was vindicated. The selective girl was clearly the most popular of the five, being chosen and liked more than any of her competitors.

These studies indicate that a person who is selectively reticent on first being approached for a date is seen as more attractive. But the idea of playing hard to get, as we normally think of it, goes well beyond the first contact. Formally stated, it means that if we have expended a great deal of time and energy in persuading somebody that we are worthy to be their romantic partner, our own love for them is likely to be more intense and longer lasting as a result. Perhaps the unconscious logic runs along these lines: 'I have worked very hard to secure the affection of this person, therefore he (she) must be an exceptional person and/or I love her very much.'

There are numerous experiments which confirm the general principle that the more you work for something, the more you appreciate attaining it. One example is an experiment concerned with selecting students to join a professional training course. Half the students were put through a rigorous selection procedure involving gruelling tests and interviews; the others were simply told details about the course. All the students were accepted for training, and subsequent ratings revealed that the former group had found the course more enjoyable. The belief that entry was highly coveted and selective apparently produced a more positive attitude towards the course. A classic corollary to this logic was expressed by Groucho Marx when he said, 'I would never join any club that would accept me as a member.'

Other relevant experiments were discussed under the heading of the 'gain phenomenon' in the last chapter. Initial coolness towards a new acquaintance may cause them to view you as sincere and discriminating in the expression of affection, or confident and much in social demand. This tilts the balance of respect and self-esteem in such a way that subsequent civility and warmth is greeted with relief and gratitude. All in all, there seems to be sufficient basis to conclude that playing hard to get can be effective in evoking stronger feelings of love in a suitor, provided he regards the pursuit as worthwhile and that he is not discouraged to the extent that he gives up the chase prematurely.

Emotional arousal as a catalyst to love

Of all the factors conducive to the development of passionate and romantic love, the one that has emerged most clearly and consistently in the research is that of emotional arousal. It does not seem to matter very much whether the arousing experience is of a positive nature (e.g. excitement or success arising out of amateur dramatics, mountain climbing, or passing an examination) or basically unpleasant (e.g. danger, fear, pain), but ideally it should occur as a shared emotional experience.

A classic series of experiments by Stanley Schachter of Columbia University, New York, showed that people who had been rendered anxious in an experimental situation developed a strong tendency toward affiliation with others in a similar plight. In one study, female students who were strangers to each other were required to take part in an experiment on the physiological effects of electric shock. Half the women were told the shocks would be painful, although not causing permanent tissue damage. The other half were told the shocks would only produce a ticklish or tingling sensation. During a ten minute wait before the experiment the women completed a questionnaire, one of the questions asking whether they would prefer to wait by themselves or in a classroom with other subjects. Twice as many students in the high anxiety group chose to wait with someone else who was in the same predicament.

This experiment indicates that people seek human contact when feeling anxious. There is also evidence that anxiety increases sexual arousal. In an important experiment by Donald Dutton and Arthur Aron of the University of British Columbia, Vancouver, men were tested on two types of bridge – a fear-arousing suspension bridge and an ordinary bridge. The suspension bridge overlooked a 230 foot drop onto rocks below and swayed dangerously so that people had to walk across slowly, clasping onto a low hand-rail. Male traversers were approached by an attractive female interviewer who asked them to fill in questionnaires. The sexual content of their answers was greater on the suspension bridge. Also, the interviewer gave the men her

Anxiety related to affiliation

	Choose to mix	Don't care	Choose to be alone
High anxiety	20	9	3
Low anxiety	10	18	2

In Schachter's famous experiment, subjects waiting to take part in an experiment on electrical shocks were given the choice of waiting alone or in a waiting room with others in the same predicament. Most of the subjects who had been made highly anxious chose to wait with others. (from Schachter 1969)

phone number saying she would be happy to give them further details about the study. Significantly more of the men on the suspension bridge attempted subsequent contact with her.

Apparently fear is conducive to attraction and love, a point which may partly explain the striking increase in romances during the war years, as well as the widespread belief that illicit love affairs are more rewarding than socially sanctioned ones.

The attribution theory of love

Schachter's work has led to an interesting theory as to why emotional arousal is conducive to falling in love. It seems that the experience of any given emotion involves two separate stages. The first is the experience of physiological arousal (e.g. a quickened breath, a beating heart), and the second is the labelling of the arousal as a particular emotion, such as anger, fear, or love. The rules for this labelling are learned from other people, both directly and through the mass media. Thus a person will experience love only if (1) he is physiologically aroused, and (2) he concludes that love is the appropriate label for his arousal feelings.

Support for attribution theory in general comes from experiments in which subjects are injected with adrenalin (a drug which produces a general arousal reaction). The emotional experience that they describe is found to depend upon their cognitive appraisal of the situation, e.g. what effect they expect the drug to have and the way in which other people supposedly on the drug are seen to behave.

Sexual arousal would seem to be particularly well-placed to be labelled (mis-labelled?) as 'love', which might explain why both sexual gratification and frustration have been cited by different theorists as conducive to romantic love. What at first sight seems like a direct contradiction is easily accounted for by attribution theory. A person who is aroused in the presence of an attractive partner either because sexual consummation is blocked or because gratification has been obtained may under appropriate circumstances classify his (her) emotion as love.

Stuart Valins of the University of North Carolina has shown that even the erroneous belief that a woman has excited a man can facilitate his attraction for her. Male college students were given false feedback concerning their heart rate as they looked at a series of semi-nude photographs selected from *Playboy* magazine. For some of the slides the heart rate was heard to increase, while for others there was no reaction. When the men were subsequently asked to rate how attractive the girls in the pictures were they markedly preferred the ones they thought had aroused them. This effect was found to persist even when they were interviewed again a month later in a totally different context.

The attribution theory has proved itself capable of accommodating a great variety of experimental findings and intuitive observations about love. The facilitating effects of parental obstruction, forced separation, rejection, fear, and excitement can all be subsumed under this theory. Even perversions such as masochism can be partly comprehended in this light, as well as revitalising effects of lovers' tiffs. Certainly, no other theory seems capable of explaining why the sensation that we call love can incorporate elements of emotions as far apart as grief, jealousy, fear and joy. It is also difficult to imagine any other theory which could explain why such a wide variety of arousing experiences have the capacity to fuel romantic passion.

Falling out of love

If falling in love is a highly emotional process, at least an equal amount of turmoil may be experienced over the termination of a love affair. In a report to the 1975 American Psychological Association Annual Convention, Dorothy Tennov of Bridgeport University described the extent of pain and suffering that is associated with various stages of love relationships. Responses to a questionnaire by a group of single men and women aged 17 to 26 revealed that 60 per cent had been severely depressed at some time over love, and 25 per cent had contemplated suicide. Especially when getting over a broken love affair the respondents agreed that they felt insecure, depressed and had great difficulty in social relations. Many also expressed guilt and

Major reasons for breaking off romances

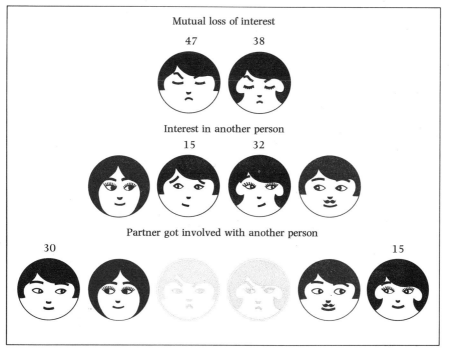

Women appear to be more active in breaking off love affairs than men. The most common reason for ending a romance unilaterally is involvement with another person; both males and females agree that this happens more often to the woman.
(from Kirkpatrick and Caplow 1945)

concern over having to reject someone. In contrast, the loss of a friend did not engender any comparable degree of suffering.

The most detailed study of the effects of broken romances was done some years ago by the American sociologists Clifford Kirkpatrick and Theodore Caplow. Several hundred students were asked to report on the frequency of their broken love affairs, the length of time it took them to readjust, and the symptoms of perseveration that they had noted. On average the students reported about two broken romances each, with little difference between men and women in this respect. About half of all engagements entered into during the college years were broken.

Mutual loss of interest was given as the main reason for the break-up of a relationship by 47 per cent of men and 38 per cent of women. Presumably, for these students little distress was entailed. In more than half of the cases, however, unilateral reasons were given for the breakup. The women were more likely to have broken it off because of an interest in someone else (32 per cent as against 15 per cent of men), which is consistent with the fact that twice as many men cited the partner's interest in another person as the prime cause of the breakup (30 per cent as against 15 per cent). This runs contrary to the popular view of the female as the victim of heartless male infidelity; where a unilateral decision is taken to break off a romance, it is apparently more often the female who takes it. La donna è mobile!

About half of the students felt no ill effects following the end of their relationship, and were able to readjust virtually immediately. No doubt these were mostly the ones who had undergone a mutual loss

Reactions of students to broken love affairs

	Males (%)	Females (%)
Frequenting places with common associations	11	10
Avoiding places with common associations	3	3
Avoiding meetings	5	5
Attempting meetings	6	4
Remembering only pleasant things	16	16
Remembering only unpleasant things	2	4
Dreaming about partner	16	11
Daydreaming	14	11
Imagining recognition	6	8
Liking or disliking people because of resemblance	6	5
Imitating mannerisms	2	2
Preserving keepsakes	7	11
Reading over old letters	7	9

Love is not always a positive thing. Especially when unrequited or after the break up of a romance, it is responsible for a great deal of distress. Many people take years to regain their earlier equilibrium. (from Kirkpatrick and Caplow 1945)

of interest. Many others, however (presumably those who were victims of a unilateral decision to break it off), experienced a great deal of unhappiness. A considerable amount of unadaptive behaviour occurred, such as frequenting places with common associations and reading over old letters. There were also some effects on mental life. Men reported dreaming and fantasising about their ex-partner more than women, which is interesting because it might reflect the fact that men are more visually (Eros) orientated. Pleasant things about the relationship were dwelt upon much more than unpleasant aspects and episodes. Rather than being adaptive or defensive, this could paradoxically be all the more painful because happiness is to some extent judged relative to past happiness. The women took slightly longer to get over their broken romances than men, and a certain proportion of people took a very long time. Seven per cent of men and 11 per cent of women required a year or more to readjust.

The experience of losing a lover has a great deal in common with bereavement, but there are some ways in which it may be worse. When a loved one dies the end is final and decisive. Lovers, on the other hand, often feel a great deal of conflict about whether or not they should try to reconstruct their relationship or win back their lost partner. They may feel the pain of repeated failure in their attempts to do this. There is also a loss of self-esteem involved in being thrown over by a partner which is not present with bereavement. Altogether, the pain and suffering for which Cupid is sometimes responsible is comparable to the joy that he at other times provides.

5

The chemistry of love

'The chemistry just wasn't right' said a girl to her room-mate in explaining why she had broken up with her latest boyfriend somewhat perfunctorily. But what exactly did she mean? And what has chemistry to do with sexual attraction? Surely it is only concerned with molecular bonds, not the molar bonds of love. In fact, many chemicals influence our sexual interests and behaviour. Some of them, hormones, are produced inside our own bodies according to environmental conditions and instructions contained in our chromosomes; others, called pheromones, are produced by other people and detected by our chemical sensors, smell and taste. Others, like aphrodisiacs, are taken in through our mouth and enter the blood stream through the stomach wall. In each case, these chemical agents are capable of influencing our sexual experience and behaviour.

Testosterone: the devil in Miss Jones
Sex hormones are chemicals released by the gonads and other glands which circulate through the blood back to the brain where, in some way that we don't yet fully understand, they influence our biological readiness for reproduction, attractiveness to potential partners and receptiveness to them. It is widely thought that male sexuality is determined by the hormone called testosterone while female sexuality is controlled by oestrogen, but this is very much an over-simplification. In primates at least, the 'male' hormone testosterone is largely responsible for the libido or sex drive of females as well as males. In other words, women are sexually assertive only in so far as they share male hormones to some extent. Testosterone in the female is produced mainly by the outer part of the adrenal glands but also by the ovaries. Female monkeys deprived of these glands are totally unreceptive to male advances but injections of testosterone restore their interest. Similarly, testosterone is known to increase libido in human females. Further injections of the male hormone in normal men have no effect, however, because they are already above a kind of saturation level.

It is widely believed, despite the current women's movement, that men have higher sex drives on average than women. Certainly, it is much easier to attract men to orgies and porno movie shows than it is women, and many more men than women engage in promiscuous sexual liaisons. Very probably this reflects the fact that men have more testosterone coursing about in their blood — hence the expression 'hot-blooded male'. In a later chapter, we note that male homosexuals are frequently found to have testosterone levels so low that they are outside the range of those of normal males. It is difficult to assess the causal significance of this observation, however; raising their testosterone level artificially is more likely to increase their homosexual urges than change their orientation in the heterosexual direction. Apparently testosterone has the effect of increasing whatever sex urges are already present, whether they be male or female, homosexual or heterosexual, orthodox or perverted.

Testosterone and aggression
Psychoanalysts have long stressed the connection between sex and aggression, often using the term libido to encompass both motives. More specifically, it is thought that *male* sexuality is linked with aggression, while female sexuality is somehow associated with or enhanced by passivity and domination by the male. In other words, it is felt that men make better sadists and women have a natural inclination towards masochism.

A variety of observations have been marshalled to support this notion, ranging from the sexual behaviour of animals to the masturbatory fantasies of men and women. Recurrent themes in literature and entertainment have also been cited. There seems to be something archetypal about the situation that occurs in Puccini's opera *Tosca* in which the wicked nobleman Scarpia offers a safe conduct to Tosca and her boyfriend, who is being tortured for political reasons, in return for her sexual favour. She is appalled by his bestiality yet cannot help being fascinated by him at the same time and this makes her doubly sick when she stabs him to death after the release has been signed. In Benjamin Britten's *Rape of Lucretia*, Collatinus attempts to reassure his wife that her violation can be forgotten, but she finally commits suicide, not because she has been raped by Tarquinius, but rather out of guilt at having enjoyed it so much. A similar kind of fascination is frequently felt in watching horror films. In the story of Dracula, for example, the aristocratic vampire is ostensibly thirsting after blood and is the personification of evil. Yet, especially as portrayed by Christopher Lee in the Hammer Films series, his sex appeal is undeniable.

This connection between aggression and sex probably comes

about because the male sex hormone testosterone predisposes towards aggression as well as sex drive. It is now established that violent criminals are inclined to have higher levels of testosterone than non-violent criminals (e.g. men convicted of fraud) or non-prisoners. Castration is known to reduce aggressiveness in adult men, particularly those with abnormally high drive levels such as persistent sex offenders and violent criminals. Social role learning is not an adequate explanation of the differences between men and women for they apply to all mammals — the males are more aggressive and their aggressiveness is dependent upon circulating testosterone.

It is frequently suggested that male aggressiveness is necessary in any species because the male has to apply brute force to effectively rape the female; i.e. it is said to enable him to pursue her successfully and hold her down until he has discharged his duty. This is almost certainly not true. For a start, receptive females do not usually need to be raped by their males; if anything, it tends to be the other way about. 'Hell hath no fury like a woman scorned' applies in the animal and human world equally. The real function of aggression is more likely found in its relevance to the job of hunting and defending the family or species against attack, selection for this capability taking place when males compete within their species for positions in a dominance hierarchy which determines access to the females. In other words, male aggression has not evolved for the purpose of giving the male direct dominance over the female; it gives dominance over rival males and thus enhances attractiveness to the female. We have seen earlier that something parallel to this primate observation does occur with humans, although dominance depends more on factors such as intelligence, achievement and money than direct physical strength.

The female cycle

The menstrual cycle is controlled mainly by the female hormones oestrogen and progesterone. Most non-primate animals restrict their sexual activity to a brief period of fertility and receptivity in the middle of the cycle, presumably because oestrogen is in primary control of their mating behaviour. The primates including man are, however, always receptive because testosterone, which is continuously secreted throughout the female cycle, is a more important determinant of their sexual behaviour.

Testosterone levels are highest around the time of ovulation (maximum fertility), and female monkeys, at least, are most receptive at this time. After ovulation, progesterone is released which acts to inhibit the secretion of testosterone and sex drive is thus diminished. There is still a great deal of argument as to whether women also experience heightened libido around the time of ovulation. From an evolutionary standpoint, it would be surprising if this mechanism were not operative in humans since it has obvious reproductive advantages. Yet studies conducted before 1950 appeared to show that maximum libido in women occurs just before and after menstruation, i.e. the times of lowest fertility. Probably the confounding factor was awareness of the so-called 'safe-period'. Only humans know that intercourse around the time of menstruation is unlikely to result in pregnancy; since the index of female libido was usually taken as the amount of sexual activity at various times in the cycle, any subjects who were deliberately practising this 'Vatican roulette' (and many did before the advent of modern contraception) would be throwing the results of the experiment enormously. Recent researchers claim to have observed the more predictable mid-cycle elevation of sexual interest in women.

Also relevant to this issue is the question of personality changes through the menstrual cycle. There is now little doubt that women are at their best physically and psychologically during ovulation; their performance on tasks such as typing is at peak during this time and they are more often euphoric and elated in mood. By contrast, many women experience depression and irritability (the so-called 'pre-menstrual tension') shortly before their menstruation begins and a greater amount of anti-social and erratic behaviour such as shoplifting and suicide occurs during menstruation.

Behaviour can affect hormone levels

While it is clear that hormones can affect behaviour, it also seems that behaviour and experience can affect hormone levels. Presumably, this is because hormone secretion is controlled by the pituitary or 'master' gland, which has connections with the hypothalamus in the brain. Testosterone levels are likely to increase with exposure to sexually arousing stimuli such as pornographic movies and the proximity of beautiful women. On the other hand, fear, stress and anxiety can cause testosterone to diminish in concentration, leading in some cases to impotence or frigidity. Nothing could better illustrate the extent to which our psychology and chemistry are interdependent and the potentially vicious circles that are possible.

Social circumstances have been shown to affect the course of a woman's cycle. A recent study by Martha McClintock, of Harvard University, found that a group of women living together in a dormitory showed a progressive trend towards synchrony of their cycles. The longer they lived together, the more their periods tended to occur on the same days, even though most of the women claimed they were not aware of when the others were menstruating. Another interesting discovery was that those girls who were frequently going out with men tended to have shorter cycles and more reliable periods. The author interpreted these findings as reflecting the effects of two pheromones; one released by other girls causing synchronisation of the cycles and one produced by their boy friends leading to a shortening and stabilisation of the cycle. The latter interpretation is particularly dubious since it is likely that sexual activity could directly affect the cycles of the girls with male contact. For example, the act of intercourse could lead to a release of hormones which hastens the occurrence of ovulation, thus shortening the cycle; this certainly occurs in non-human animals and has obvious evolutionary significance in that it increases the chances of pregnancy occurring.

Pheromones: a taste of honey
Pheromones are substances emitted by an animal which have the effect of attracting or stimulating a potential mate. Their mechanism is well established in non-human species. Rams will mount pregnant ewes that have been annointed with vaginal secretions from oestrus ewes; otherwise they would be distinctly disinterested. Homosexual hamsters can be created in the same way. The power of female genital odours to attract males of the same species has also been demonstrated in rats, cows and monkeys and preparations are commercially available which are supposed to prevent oestrus bitches from attracting male dogs.

Production of female pheromones is under the control of the hormone oestrogen. Female monkeys, for example, produce a collection of fatty acids, called copulins, which are alluring to the male; they appear in highest concentration around the time of ovulation and fall off towards menstruation as a result of increased secretion of progesterone (the female hormone which inhibits both testosterone and oestrogen production and is an important component of the contraceptive pill). Scientists in Atlanta have recently discovered a similar range of fatty acids in the human female which show the same cyclic variation in concentration as the monkey copulins. While their attractiveness to men has not been directly demonstrated, we cannot rule out the possibility that the popularity of oral-genital contact as a preamble to sexual intercourse is related to the presence of such chemical attractants.

We are not generally conscious of being attracted by the smells emitted by our sex partners, though we are certainly aware of our repulsion when they smell bad. As a result, the cosmetics manufacturers have done very well out of deodorants, mouthwashes, vaginal sprays and suchlike, which are designed to eliminate or disguise unpleasant body odours. Nevertheless, many people do report being turned on by the smell of their partner's sweat or other body odours, and it may be that these commercial preparations are sometimes self-defeating in that they interfere with the desirable effects of nature's own perfumes. In Mediterranean countries there are dances in which the men wave little handkerchiefs in front of the girls of their choice, having earlier worn them under the armpits to impregnate them with their smell. It has also been found that women can perceive certain musk substances that men are unable to smell unless injected with the female hormone oestrogen; and women's sensitivity to these musks varies with their fertility cycle. It therefore seems likely that men give off similar smells without being aware of it. Musk is actually a pheromone produced by the male deer for the purpose of attracting the female; the logic of incorporating it in women's perfumes is somewhat peculiar.

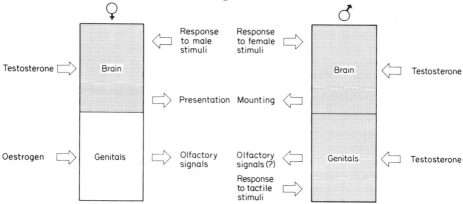

Hormones and sexual behavior

In women, testosterone is believed to act on the brain to increase interest in sexual activity, while oestrogen produces vaginal secretions which are attractive to men, particularly around the time of ovulation. In men, testosterone acts on both brain and genitals to influence directly their response to visual and tactile sex stimuli in the environment. (from *New Scientist*, 6 February 1975)

The importance of pheromones for human sexual attraction has not been directly demonstrated, then, but there is good reason to suspect that they are still operative, albeit at a subliminal level. Reverse pheromone effects, i.e. the capacity of certain body odours to repulse potential sex partners, are well acknowledged and cosmetics may have rational use in the removal and masking of some of these.

Aphrodisiacs

Several years ago, a nineteen year old university student in New Zealand was handed a small package of white crystals by an older student with the advice that it was Spanish Fly, the famous love potion supposed to render women helpless with sexual desire. Not unnaturally, he slipped some into the coffee of the girl he was dating at the time to see how she would respond. Within an hour or so she had died in agony with severe internal bleeding and her boyfriend was subsequently sentenced to five years in prison for manslaughter.

This tragic incident underscores the ignorance that prevails in society today as to what substances are and are not effective aphrodisiacs. Spanish Fly, otherwise cantharidin, is not so much a love potion as a deadly poison. Applied externally to the genitals of a male horse, it produces an irritation that may be misinterpreted by the beast as sexual excitement. Taken internally by a woman in very, very low concentrations, it may irritate the urethra and produce a similar effect. But even a few crystals in a cup of coffee can be fatal to the consumer. It is time that the truth about Spanish Fly was properly publicised.

Also unfounded are the reputations of caviar, oysters and vitamin E, although these are all good foods which have positive general effects upon health and vitality. Some time ago, it was reported that vitamin E, which is found in grain husks (and thus wholemeal bread) caused rats persistently to attempt to climb out of their cages to reach female rats. A human parallel was thought to have been discovered when Olympic athletes on vitamin supplemented diets were observed to climb high wire fences in order to get to the female quarters; it was subsequently acknowledged, however, that such behaviour was not without precedent in the history of athletic meets. Thus evidence for the specific rejuvenating and stimulating properties of vitamin E, as apart from its general health value, is still lacking.

Alcohol is the most widely used drug in our society that has any claim to aphrodisiac properties. But its blessings are definitely mixed. According to Macbeth's gate porter 'it provokes the desire, but it takes away the performance'. Actually, it doesn't so much increase libido as remove inhibitions (part of its general depressant action on the brain) but in doing so, it will increase the chances of sexual congress taking place up until the point where the ability to perform, particularly of the male, has been destroyed. Fortunately there is a distinct breakdown of inhibitions for most people well before this stage is reached. Some psychoanalysts have light-heartedly defined the superego as that part of the psyche that dissolves in alcohol.

Marijuana (cannabis) is a drug that has similar advantages and disadvantages to alcohol but is complicated by legal restrictions in most countries. Mescaline is better than either in that it induces euphoria rather than sleepiness as well as releasing the taker from inhibitions. In fact, considering the absence of unpleasant side-effects, mescaline, in mild doses, is probably the best all-round aphrodisiac yet to have been discovered. Perhaps for this reason, it is likely to remain illegal for a long time. Society much prefers drugs like alcohol and nicotine which incorporate their own punishments for excessive use. Psilocybin and LSD are drugs which have very similar effects to mescaline, but the latter in particular is dosage-critical and has certain dangers associated with it.

None of the above is a true aphrodisiac; their effect is to counter inhibition rather than heighten sex drive. Although the quest has been about as ardent as that for the philosopher's stone, no drug with this general capability has yet come to light. We have seen that testosterone may heighten libido in men who are deficient in it for some reason, but it will not increase sex drive in normal men. Male hormones can increase sex drive in women but among the unfortunate side-effects is the possibility that they will develop secondary masculine characteristics such as a deep voice and hair on the chin. Another limitation of hormone therapy for sexual inadequacy of the impotence/frigidity type is that it will not help in the fairly high proportion of cases in which the lack of receptiveness is specific to a particular person such as the spouse. Thus, if testosterone is administered to a husband who has acquired a conditioned aversion to his wife as a result of several years of rancid quarrelling it will either have no effect on his sexual inclinations or else cause him to pursue his office girls with greater fervour; what it cannot do is alter his basic attitude towards his wife.

Isolated reports of drugs producing aphrodisiac effects with clinical patients have appeared from time to time. One of the best known concerns a drug called l-dopa which is used in the treatment of Parkinson's Disease. Geriatric patients treated with this drug have shown astounding rejuvenation and, in some cases, have been observed to pursue amorously young nurses on the wards. L-dopa has certain negative side-effects, however, and it is not believed to increase sexual excitement in young, healthy persons.

A few years ago, John Doust and Louis Huszka of the Clarke Institute of Psychiatry in Toronto reported that a particular combination of drugs (l-tryptophan, an anti-depressant and a tranquilliser with anti-serotonin and adrenalytic properties) provoked compulsive sexual behaviour in some female schizophrenic patients. 'In three patients, sexual activity was definitely exaggerated: male cleaning staff entering the ward would be greeted by seductive behaviour; one patient with a quiescent, incestuous relationship with her father, became demanding in her insistence in again pursuing this end; two patients repeatedly climbed into bed together and were observed kissing each other and petting. The remaining two patients developed compulsive pathological sexual activation: one of these patients frequently smeared lipstick in grotesque fashion on her face; both would sexually assault male cleaners when they visited the ward, both would expose themselves, dance and prance around the floor in a sexually provocative fashion and make sexual demands upon nurses and fellow patients; both would masturbate openly as well as covertly when no opportunity to involve another person offered itself.'

A plain man's guide to aphrodisiacs

Reputed aphrodisiacs	Known effects
Cantharidin (Spanish Fly)	Irritation of urethra; possibly death
Vitamin E	None established in humans
Caviar; oysters	None
Alcohol; marijuana	Reduction of inhibition; possible performance loss
Mescaline; psilocybin	Reduction of inhibition; euphoria
L-dopa	Rejuvenation of some Parkinson's Disease patients
Testosterone	Increased libido in women and men with deficiency
Brand X (see text)	Striking results with schizophrenic women

Assuming that these effects are not unique to schizophrenic patients, the researchers really seem to have stumbled over a preparation with commercial possibilities. However, we are not aware of any further developments with this recipe and so it seems we must content ourselves for some time to come with the imperfect approximations that are currently available.

Anti-aphrodisiacs

Generally, it is a great deal easier to turn people off than to turn them on, but few people complain about being over-sexed so there is little demand for such an agent. Several different techniques have been used for reducing libido in persistent sex offenders, most of whom are male for reasons mentioned earlier. The crudest method is, of course, castration – a highly effective way of eliminating testosterone from the bloodstream, but rather drastic and irreversible. Oestrogens and tranquillisers have also shown some efficacy in reducing sexual desire, but both have side-effects. Oestrogens may cause nausea, enlargement of the breasts and increase the risk of thrombosis; tranquillisers are likely to cause drowsiness and depression. Recently, a drug called cyproterone has been used with a great deal of success; this blocks the action of testosterone without any unpleasant side-effects and seems to be the preferred method for reducing sex drive.

The use of such treatments with sex offenders raises obvious ethical and practical problems. How can we be sure that submission to treatment is voluntary in the case of a long term prisoner? Usually, prisoners are told that successful treatment will not shorten their sentence, only decrease the chances of them finding themselves in similar trouble again. Nevertheless, it must be easy for them to believe that treatment might result in an earlier release and tempting for the authorities to be influenced by it. Does this amount to a form of coercion? Once out of prison, there is the question of whether the offender will stick to his drug regimen or allow his old urges to reassert themselves. This is why castration has been preferred as a treatment in several, particularly Scandinavian, countries; its effect is much more permanent and reliable. In San Diego, for example, there have been 397 castrations of sex criminals and the operation appears to have been successful in keeping all the men out of further trouble.

Cigarette smoking is also an anti-aphrodisiac; as long ago as 1622, Sultan Mourach forbade the use of tobacco on grounds that it adversely affected virility, and it now seems that he was right. The Australian biochemist, Michael Briggs, has shown that when men give up smoking, there is a rise in the level of testosterone in the blood. In Hungary, Dr Mihaly Viczian discovered a lower sperm count and a higher proportion of malformed sperm in male smokers compared to non-smokers, though he did not think the difference was sufficient to consider smoking a cause of sterility. Further corroboration comes from two French doctors who asked a large group of elderly men to report retrospectively on their sex lives; the heavy smokers among them claimed significantly less sexual activity between the ages of 25 and 40. Although this finding could be interpreted as meaning that non-smokers are more boastful concerning their sexual prowess, the weight of evidence does indicate that smoking is slightly inhibitory to sexual potency.

Hormone replacement therapy

At around the age of 50 there is a distinct slow-down in the production of oestrogen from women's ovaries. As a result, they stop having periods and become infertile. This change of life is often also associated with depression, hot sweats, drying of the vagina and loss of interest in sex. Oestrogen replacement therapy goes quite a long way towards preventing these symptoms, though some doctors are reluctant to prescribe it because of possible side effects. There is apparently an increased risk of blood-clotting (cf. the contraceptive pill) and gall bladder disease.

As we have said, testosterone supplements may be effective in restoring the sex drive of castrated males but have little effect on normal men. This is because of the threshold effect that is seen with many hormones; a certain level is necessary for a function to be operative, after which further increases in level count for very little. For this reason it is in older men, whose level has dropped below the threshold, that replacement therapy may be indicated. Apparently there is less risk of side-effects with testosterone in males than there is for either testosterone or oestrogen in females. Testosterone is fairly widely prescribed for elderly businessmen in the United States, but has yet to become popular in Europe.

As indicated in this chapter there is no really effective aphrodisiac for general use. Stopping smoking, taking an interest in erotica and trying to improve one's general health may all help to a limited extent and are all that can be confidently recommended. With regard to improving physical fitness, studies on the effects of regular exercise in middle-aged men have invariably failed to reveal any of the expected benefits, such as increased resistance to infection or stress. Many of the men in these experiments, however, have reported an improvement in their sex life. Additional evidence for the effects of exercise on sex drive comes from an ongoing questionnaire study of the Great Britain track and field team. These internationals score above average on ambition and aggression as expected, but they score even higher on 'interest in sex'. However, since most men would consider taking an early morning run round the local park to be too drastic a step to take in the interests of their libido, the optimistic search for a true aphrodisiac is bound to continue.

6

Homosexuality and other variations

So far, we have discussed sexual attraction and love as though they only occur between opposite-sex adults of approximately the same age and attractiveness. Statistically, and perhaps also biologically, this is the norm. But there are also a lot of variations as regards the prime target of people's interest. There are variations from time to time within any one person as to precisely what has the greatest arousal potential and there are also fairly stable differences between people in their sexual orientations. The most widespread and best known of these variations is homosexuality.

How common is homosexuality?

Homosexuality has been identified in most cultures — primitive and advanced, classical and modern. Ancient Greece is frequently cited as a civilisation in which homosexual love flourished and was to some extent ennobled; it was endorsed by some of the great philosophers such as Plato and the admiration of the young male athlete, in particular, emerges clearly in the sculpture and art of the time. In imperial Rome, homosexuality was apparently also quite common but not held in such esteem; instead, it was viewed as another aspect of the corruption and debauchery which signalled the decline of Rome. Many societies, including our own in recent times, have attempted to suppress homosexuality by laws and sanctions, but they have never been very successful in doing so.

The largest census of homosexuality ever undertaken was that of Kinsey and his co-workers in the 1940s and 1950s. They found that about 4 per cent of men are exclusively homosexual throughout their lives after the onset of adolescence and as many as a quarter have more than incidental homosexual experience. Considering the extent of public revulsion against homosexuality at the time of this survey, it is unlikely to be an underestimate of the current state of affairs. Homosexuality was found among all social and occupational groups, and the incidence of homosexual experience was as high as 50 per cent in men who had remained bachelors until the age of 35. Surveys conducted since Kinsey have generally tended to support these rough estimates; despite the strength of the taboo against it, a fairly high proportion of men have had some kind of homosexual contact.

With women, the situation is strikingly different. Although the social taboos are, if anything, less strong than they are for men, less than one third as many women engage in homosexual behaviour. Whereas 37 per cent of men have had some kind of homosexual experience leading to orgasm since adolescence, according to Kinsey, the comparable figure for women is only 13 per cent. Only 3 per cent of women report having been primarily homosexual at any time in their lives (compared to 10 per cent of men) and only about 1 per cent of women are exclusively homosexual throughout life. Some possible reasons for this lower incidence of homosexuality in women are presented later in the chapter.

What do homosexuals actually do with each other?

Most 'gay' men engage in a variety of sexual behaviour although each individual usually has one preferred mode of sexual expression. The most popular activities are mutual masturbation and fellatio, but anal intercourse is also quite common. Lesbians tend to favour manual stimulation of the clitoris, cunnilingus and intercourse with the aid of a dildo occurring with less frequency. Contrary to the belief of many people, sado-masochistic activity is not at all popular with homosexuals; probably it occurs no more frequently in homosexual than heterosexual relationships. Some homosexuals are fixated on either the dominant or passive role to the exclusion of the other, but it is much more common for the couple to take turn about and experience both ends of the stick, so to speak. Thus a homosexual individual will usually alternate between the active ('male') and passive ('female') roles.

The frequency of homosexual contacts is much greater for gay men than gay women. The men tend to be very promiscuous, preferring a high turnover of casual partners. It has been estimated that the average homosexual man has 1,000 partners in the course of a lifetime, most of them strangers prior to the encounter and with whom sex is had only once. Only a few of their relationships entail any degree of care and affection. This compares with the typical heterosexual man, who has about ten partners in his lifetime and enters into some kind of personal relationship with the majority of them. This promiscuity is a major reason why homosexual men are highly susceptible to venereal diseases (most forms of VD can be transmitted by anal intercourse as well as normal intercourse). Gay women have fewer relationships, most of them relatively long-term and involving a degree of commitment and affection – perhaps comparable to the life style of heterosexual women.

There is a great deal of variation in the frequency with which homosexuals have sex. In Alan Bell's Californian sample, 16 per cent of white males reported that they engaged in sexual activity of some kind with a partner four or more times per week on average. An equal proportion reported having sex only once a month or less. Homosexuals are often accused of having an exceptionally high preoccupation with sex. Bell's data indicate that the level of sexual interest in homosexuals is actually *lower* than that of heterosexual men. As many as 18 per cent of gay men claimed that they hardly thought about sex at all during the course of the day. How many 'straight' men could say this in all honesty? We will see later that the hormone evidence provides some support for this survey-based claim of low sex drive in homosexual men.

Female homosexuals engage in much less overt sexual behaviour than their male counterparts. Male homosexuals begin masturbating much earlier than the females and continue to do so more often, even when involved in an active relationship with a boy friend.

'Cruising' is the term used to denote going out to look for a casual partner. The most popular pick-up places are gay bars, steam baths, streets, private parties, parks, beaches, public lavatories and movie theatres. Different types of gay men have different preferred hunting grounds. For example, the young, attractive, overt and exclusive homosexual characteristically finds his contacts at gay bars and saunas where he is immersed in the gay subculture and enters into competition for the most desirable partners. Those who frequent public toilets, on the other hand, are often predominantly heterosexual, married men whose homosexual side-line is unknown to their wives or other people.

Homosexuality and effeminacy

There is a widely-held stereotype in our society of the homosexual as a limp-wristed, mincing, lisping 'fairy'. Like most stereotypes, there is at least an element of truth in it; a certain proportion of male homosexuals do exhibit various kinds of effeminate behaviour. In order to investigate this question, four psychiatrists at the Harvard Medical School constructed a rating scale for assessing effeminacy based on items such as those given below. A group of sixteen well-adjusted homosexual men scored twice as high on average as a control group of heterosexuals. However, there were wide variations within each of these groups and a considerable amount of overlap between them. The average number of items checked as effeminate for the homosexual group was only seven. Thus, while there is an increased chance of a homosexual man displaying feminine characteristics, there are very few that conform to the stereotype completely and very many who are just as masculine as any man.

Effeminacy rating scale

Speech
1   Do you speak with a high voice (a consistently high tone or occasional falsetto)?
2   Does your voice trail off in the midst of or at the ends of a sentence?
3   Do you use nouns in a bizarre diminutive fashion (e.g. 'drinkie' or even 'drinkie-pooh' for drink)?

Gait
4   Do you walk in small mincing steps?
5   Do your thighs rub together when you walk?
6   As you walk, do your buttocks noticeably roll in an up-and-down direction?

Posture
7   When you sit, do you double-cross your legs, that is, at both knee and ankle?
8   Do you display a limp wrist?
9   Do you use hands in statuesque gestures?

Mouth movements
10   Do you purse your lips when you speak?
11   Do you purse your lips when not speaking?

Upper face and eyes
12   Do you flirt with your eyes?
13   Are you furtive in terms of eye contact with an interviewer?
14   Do you raise your eyebrows for emphasis?

Body narcissism
15   Do you caress yourself (this includes face stroking and head or moustache stroking)?

Questionnaires like the one above have been used by researchers to provide a quantitative assessment of effeminacy. The more 'yes' answers you give the more effeminate you are inclined to be. A group of homosexual men scored twice as high as heterosexuals on average, though there were wide variations within each group and some overlap between them. (from Schatzberg and others 1975)

Less is known about the other side of the coin, that is, the proportion of lesbians who exhibit 'butch' characteristics, but the impression is that a similar state of affairs prevails – some, but by no means all, female homosexuals appear masculine in looks, dress and mannerisms.

What is attractive to a homosexual?

The survey by Alan Bell mentioned above also gave some information about what stimuli are exciting to the male homosexual and what he looks for in a partner. Quite a high proportion of the sample cited some fairly general and not explicitly sexual situation such as meeting a good-looking male in a social situation. Percentages of men who declared a more specific erotic stimulus, an aspect of the body, or characteristic of a desirable partner are given in the table below. The most arousing aspect of the male anatomy is apparently the chest, closely followed by the buttocks; there was also quite a bit of interest in the genitals themselves. Among the most sought-after attributes

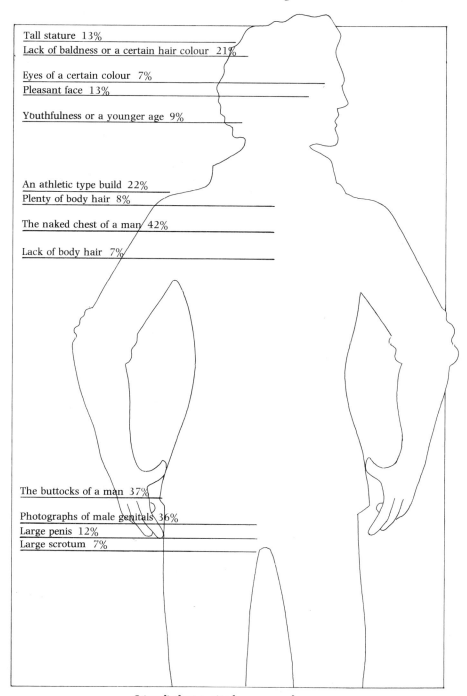

Tall stature 13%

Lack of baldness or a certain hair colour 21%

Eyes of a certain colour 7%

Pleasant face 13%

Youthfulness or a younger age 9%

An athletic type build 22%

Plenty of body hair 8%

The naked chest of a man 42%

Lack of body hair 7%

The buttocks of a man 37%

Photographs of male genitals 36%

Large penis 12%

Large scrotum 7%

Stimuli that excite homosexual men
A group of 575 white male homosexuals in the U.S. listed these stimuli as arousing
or desirable in a sex partner. (from Bell 1974)

of the ideal partner were an athletic build, lack of baldness, hair of a certain colour, a pleasant face, tall stature and a large penis.

These preferences are remarkably similar to those expressed by women when they were asked what physical characteristics of men appealed to them most (see chapter 2) — an interesting fact which might be borne in mind when we shortly come to consider theories of the nature and origins of homosexuality.

Homosexuality and marriage

It is quite common for homosexuals to marry. Oscar Wilde was a much publicised example, but more than 50 per cent of homosexuals get married at some time in their lives. F. Wafelbakker, who conducted a survey among married homosexuals in Holland, reported that some of the spouses became aware of their homosexual tendencies only after marriage, while others married in the hope of destroying their interest in their own sex. Doctors and ministers had sometimes even advocated marriage as a 'cure' for homosexuality! In some cases it was the heterosexual partner who pressed for marriage, hoping that this would dissipate the homosexual urges of his or her partner. Apart from social pressure, homosexuals often want to marry because of the hope that it will bring security, domesticity and family life — all of which are desired as much by homosexuals as by heterosexuals.

Researchers have described the typical course of a marriage that involves one homosexual partner. From the beginning, love-making is infrequent and the homosexual gradually develops a double life, having incidental homosexual encounters and adopting a cooler attitude towards the spouse. Many of the homosexuals will eventually reveal their true urges to their spouse, which usually results in a great sense of relief on both sides and a feeling of solidarity and ability to cope with the problem together. This is soon replaced, however, by doubts and mistrust on the part of the heterosexual partner. Instead of divorce, other forms of adjustment are usually made, so as to preserve the family unit, security and comradeship. The couple may opt for a platonic marriage, or a double marriage may take place, where the homosexual partner openly enters into a relationship with a third party of the same sex. 'Alternative marriage' or 'open marriage' are the terms used when both partners frankly form new relationships, sometimes even taking the new partners into the home.

What causes homosexuality?

As yet, there is no universally agreed explanation of the occurrence of homosexuality. One of the most tenacious theories, particularly of male homosexuality, is that put up by the Freudians. They are inclined to blame early childhood stresses and characteristics of the parents, particularly the combination of a dominant, overprotective mother with a weak, uninterested or absent father figure. The suggestion is that this leads to a failure of proper identification with a masculine father figure, combined with fear and abhorrence of women in general. Unfortunately, there is no satisfactory evidence to support this notion. Although there is some tendency for mothers to be nurturant towards their homosexual sons, and for fathers to be relatively cold and rejecting, the direction and cause and effect is by no means clear — most probably the parental attitudes are secondary to the discovery that they have raised a homosexual son. The psychoanalytic theory does not explain lesbianism, nor does it account for various facts about homosexuality such as its appearance in one sibling of a family but not in others, even though all the children were raised in approximately the same way by the same parents.

There is fairly strong evidence for a genetic involvement in the origin of homosexuality. In 1952, F. J. Kallmann reported on a sample of thirty-seven one-egg twins (twins having identical heredity) in which one of the twins was homosexual; in every case, the other member of the pair was also found to be homosexual. In contrast, a sample of two-egg (non-identical) twins showed less than 15 per cent concordance. Heston and Shields investigated a family of fourteen children which included three sets of identical twins; two pairs of twins were concordant for homosexuality, while both members of the third pair were heterosexual. Such data argue strongly for a genetic basis to homosexuality even though several pairs of identical twins that were not concordant for homosexuality have been discovered since the Kallmann study. Heredity is clearly involved to some extent, but does not provide a complete explanation.

Studies of the effects of hormones on animals and humans have also provided some clues as to the nature of homosexuality. It seems that around the time of birth (shortly before in the case of humans) hormones are released by the gonads which find their way back to certain brain centres (now thought to be located in a part called the hypothalamus) where they have the effect of presetting the brain for the development of a certain sexual orientation in adolescence. That is, within limits it can be said that the brain is created male or female according to the hormones that are circulating shortly before birth. Sometimes, this presetting is inappropriate in that the gender of the child is male and his anatomical appearance is male, but for some reason or another, his brain has not received the hormonal instruction that would cause it to be masculinised. This may occur either because of an excess of female hormones or an inadequate amount of the male hormone testosterone.

If the male homosexual is possessed of a female brain in certain

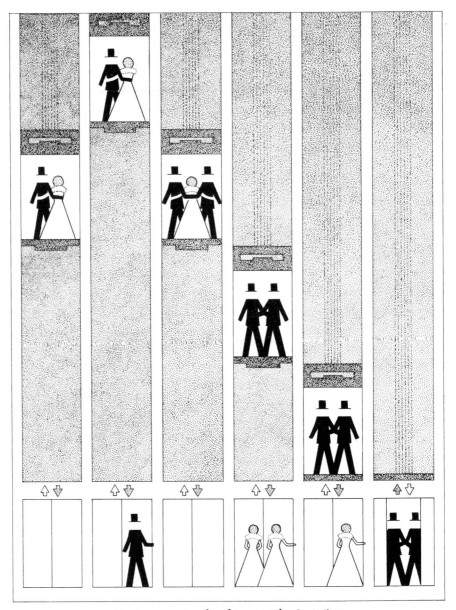

Testosterone is related to sexual orientation

Different plasma testosterone levels were found in groups of men with varying degrees of homosexuality. (from Kolodny and others 1971)

	Mean testosterone level (and S.D.) in nanograms per 100 ml	
Heterosexual controls	689	(±26)
Predominantly heterosexual but incidentally homosexual	775	(±51)
Bisexual (equally heterosexual and homosexual)	681	(±126)
Predominantly homosexual but more than incidentally heterosexual	569	(±65)
Predominantly homosexual but incidentally heterosexual	372	(±22)
Exclusively homosexual	264	(±15)

respects we might expect that the pattern of hormone release in adulthood from the pituitary gland (which is under the control of the hypothalamus) would also be affected. Early studies of hormones in homosexuals failed to detect any abnormality, but testosterone is present in the blood in very minute amounts (measured in nanograms, which are thousand millionth parts of a gram), and it is only recently that techniques sufficiently sensitive to examine the question properly have been introduced. In 1971, R. C. Kolodny, W. H. Masters and colleagues of the Harvard Medical School and Reproductive Biology Research Foundation of St Louis, Missouri, were able to detect abnormally low levels of testosterone in a group of homosexual men. Thirty student volunteers were used in the study, all of them practising homosexuals in good medical health. Blood levels of testosterone were measured and compared with those taken from fifty heterosexual men, the tests being conducted by a technician who was not told the source of the blood samples. The table below shows the average testosterone levels of the heterosexuals and homosexuals of various degrees of homosexual orientation. Those homosexuals who had little or no interest in women showed significantly lower testosterone levels than control subjects, while the bisexuals had testosterone levels that were comparable to the heterosexual controls. In addition, a high proportion of the exclusive and near-exclusive homosexuals had markedly lower sperm counts and a higher frequency of malformed sperm than controls, although none of them was actually infertile.

In another study, by J. A. Loraine and colleagues, the urine of homosexual men and women was assayed for sex hormone content. The findings were consistent with those of Kolodny in that the men had lower testosterone levels than those of heterosexual men. In addition, they found that the urine of lesbians contained a greater amount of testosterone and less oestrogen than that of heterosexual women.

Harold Lief and associates at Tulane University Medical School report an interesting case of a male who had displayed alternating cycles of male and female sex orientation between the ages of 11 and 23. The male and female phases would last for three or four days each with a transition period of a few hours during which he became very restless and tense. The characteristics of the patient during the two phases, confirmed by parents and roommate, were as follows:

Female phase
Use of name 'Evelyn Charles'
Violent attraction to one male
No attraction to women

Great number of erections and amount of sexual drive
Passive nature
Depression sometimes
Urge to 'mother' children, pets
Personality receptive to ideas, friends
Householding preoccupations, e.g. cooking, cleaning
Artistic, creative and subjective nature; concern with poetry, painting,
    nature walks, and listening to music
Higher voice
Mincing gait
Slower growth of beard

Male phase
Use of own name
No attraction to men
Weak attraction to women
Small number of erections and amount of sexual drive
Aggressive nature
Hypomania sometimes
No mothering urges
Personality rejective to ideas, argumentative, sarcastic
Intellectual preoccupations; 'keen' thinking, 'sharp' responses
Compulsive studying; objective views; concern with world affairs,
    politics, science
Lower voice
Duck-like gait
Faster growth of beard

Although it was not possible to establish directly that these phases
were associated with variations in the male/female hormone balance,
there was a great deal of indirect evidence that this had been the
case. Shortly after therapy was begun, the patient settled into a fairly
steady state which combined masculine appearance with homosexual
orientation.

Together, these studies confirm hormone abnormalities in homosexuals that are consistent with a biochemical theory of homosexuality. However, they cannot be taken as absolute proof that these
hormones are, or ever were, responsible for the homosexual behaviour. It is conceivable that a prolonged homosexual orientation
could affect the production of hormones in such a way as to yield the
results described above. That is, the altered testosterone and oestrogen
levels could be an effect rather than a cause of the homosexual interest.
The former explanation seems more likely in view of all the available
evidence, but a chicken and egg problem still has to be conceded.

The biochemical theory is unlikely to be the complete answer to the question of the origins of homosexuality. There is reason to believe that certain life experiences can also contribute to its development. Although the child-rearing studies prove very little, there is other evidence to support such a notion. Studies with rats and monkeys show that if a male animal is isolated from female company either from birth or for any appreciable period thereafter, homosexual behaviour is likely to appear. Similarly, with humans, homosexual behaviour occurs with increased frequency in situations of sexual segregation such as prisons, private boarding schools and ships. Most of the individuals concerned revert to heterosexual lives when the opposite sex becomes available again, but there is also known to be a carry-over effect for some people; some individuals acquire a taste for homosexual behaviour and continue to engage in it. Other theorists have pointed to the probable effects of imitation learning when individuals of borderline predisposition are immersed in a gay subculture; it is also likely that 'heterophobia' resulting from traumatic initial experiences with women is influential in some cases.

Almost certainly, it is necessary to think in terms of several different kinds of homosexual, the various causal factors being weighted differently for each. Male homosexuality is different from female homosexuality, exclusive homosexuality is different from bisexuality and so on; they cannot be treated as equivalent and different explanations will be required for them.

The preponderance of male over female homosexuality

One of the most clearly established facts about homosexuality is that males with such an orientation outnumber the females by a ratio of at least three to one. This is a real finding which cannot be explained away in terms of social expectations or differential secrecy. If anything, there are stronger taboos against sexual contact between males than between females; women can touch and kiss in public in a way that would really raise eyebrows if it occurred between men. Do the theories just discussed throw any light on the reasons for this male preponderance? The psychoanalytic and sociological theories do not easily account for this sex difference; males and females ought to be about equally vulnerable to family stresses and problems of sex role learning. Social isolation might possibly favour male homosexuality on the grounds that there are more situations of male segregation than female (e.g. the army, prison and certain educational institutions). However, this difference is progressively breaking down without any apparent effect on the male/female homosexuality ratio. In any case it does not seem an adequate explanation considering the extent of the difference.

Genetic and biochemical factors are, on the other hand, very well equipped to provide an explanation for this sex difference. Firstly, there is the mechanism of sex-linkage in heredity. Males are more susceptible to all forms of genetic anomaly because their Y chromosome is virtually devoid of genetic material which can offset or counterbalance peculiarities on their X chromosome. Females are fortunate in having a second X chromosome (contributed by their father) which can smooth out a lot of aberrations located on the X chromosome contributed by their mother. Certain disorders such as colour blindness, haemophilia and childhood psychosis are many times more common in men than women because their genetic basis is heavily involved with the sex chromosomes. We have established that homosexuality is partly genetic; if any of the relevant genes were located on the X chromosome (which is quite possible, however paradoxical it might sound) then we would expect the anomaly to be more common in men than women. The main argument against this explanation is that the anomaly is not really the same in male versus female homosexuality; in one case it amounts to a disposition towards female behaviour and in the other it is a disposition towards male interests and behaviour. The genetic elements involved would have fairly non-specific effects such as a general interference with foetal hormone production, male or female.

The theory which most comfortably explains the male/female ratio is the biochemical one. According to this theory, all foetuses are female until and unless the gonads release hormonal instructions to the contrary shortly before or around the time of birth. Since this means that an additional step is required to make the child a fully fledged male, another opportunity is provided for something to go wrong. In particular, what apparently sometimes happens is that the external body characteristics are converted to male form in accordance with instructions from the Y chromosome but for some reason, the relevant brain centres in the hypothalamus are not similarly transformed. It is easy to see why this pattern would occur with greater frequency than the reverse; only very occasionally would we expect freakish concentrations of male hormone to masculinise the brain areas responsible for sexual orientation without affecting any other organs. In other words, it is easier for one tiny area deep within the brain to escape the effects of testosterone than it is for all of the body *except* that area to escape. The high male to female sex ratio in homosexuality can therefore be interpreted as good support for a biochemical theory of homosexuality.

However, it is very unlikely that we have told the whole story yet. The testosterone levels for different degrees of male homosexuality reported by Kolodny suggest that exclusive homosexuality has a different biochemical basis from bisexuality. In fact, it is possible that

incidental homosexual behaviour occurring in a man who is predominantly heterosexual could result from a kind of spill-over of his
heterosexual drive. A similar theory may be used to explain the fact
that many other perversions are almost uniquely male. If we assume
that the male orientation received before birth defines a kind of ideal
target for sexual attention (the young, adult female vulva) and if we
also allow that males are highly driven sexually because of their
excessive circulating testosterone after adolescence, then we would
expect them to do a lot of 'shooting' with some of the shots scattering
around the centre of the target. Various approximations to the target
include older women, little girls, female panties and boots, and perhaps also the backside of a long-haired young man. The stronger the
sex drive, the more we would expect it to generalise around the ideal
target. Therefore, it is perhaps significant that in the table above the
highest testosterone levels occur not in the exclusive heterosexuals,
but in those that engage in occasional homosexuality as well. This
theory also fits the fact that women masturbate less than men in the
absence of an attractive partner and are less prone to adopt homosexual outlets when segregated in all-female company – their sex
drive is lower, therefore they are less versatile as regards their choice
of sex object.

This leaves us with three possible bases for the preponderance
of male homosexuality over female: (1) a sex-linkage in the genetic
basis; (2) a failure for the brain centre concerned with sex orientation
to get masculinised along with the rest of the body; (3) the higher sex
drive of males resulting in some amount of spill-over onto other
objects approximating to the ideal. Any, or more likely all, of these
factors are probably involved.

Treatment implications
What do the above theories suggest can be done about homosexuality? Quite clearly they imply that exclusive homosexuality, at
least, will be fairly resistant to any form of treatment whether
psychological or chemical. The homosexual behaviour could be
artificially suppressed by instilling strong fears and inhibitions in
connection with it, but there is no way that heterosexual interest can
be built up if its origins are prenatal and neurological. Testosterone
pills or injections are not effective because it is not the currently
circulating level of testosterone that is important, only the level
available at the time the brain is developing. Bisexuals, on the other
hand, might be steered in the heterosexual direction by social pressures, psychotherapy, or conditioning, since they already have a
degree of heterosexual interest that can be developed while attempts
are made to reduce the homosexual interest. Indeed, treatment

attempts have so far tended to fail unless the patient has some history of pleasurable heterosexual relationships; men who have been exclusively homosexual throughout life do not respond to any form of treatment.

More important is the question of whether anything *ought* to be done about homosexuality. There is no satisfactory evidence that homosexuals are psychiatrically sick; any neurotic tendencies such as the slightly increased risk of depression and anxiety that has been observed can readily be accounted for in terms of society's intolerance of their behaviour, plus the fact that more studies have been done with homosexuals who seek psychiatric help than with the high proportion who are well-adjusted and happy. With exclusive homosexuals in particular, their behaviour is perfectly natural for them and is also fairly harmless. Contrary to the belief of some, homosexuals very seldom commit sex crimes or assault small boys; if anything, they are responsible for fewer sex crimes than the high-testosterone heterosexual males (unless, of course, homosexual behaviour is itself defined as criminal). In a real sense, it could be said that it is attitude of society towards homosexuals that is sick rather than the homosexuals themselves.

Transsexualism and transvestism

Transsexualism is a special kind of homosexuality characterised by the belief held by the individual that he really belongs to the opposite sex. In the case of the male (which is again much more common than its female equivalent) he has the distinct and disturbing feeling that he is a woman trapped inside the body of a man. Frequently, this leads to demands for a sex-change operation such as removal of the male genitals and replacement with a vagina. This condition is clearly different from regular homosexuality in which the individual recognises and accepts the gender of his own body but admits that he is drawn towards members of his own sex. It is also to be distinguished from transvestism which refers to people who dress like the opposite sex but are more often than not heterosexual in their orientation. Transvestism is more like a fetish than a form of homosexuality; the transvestite is sexually aroused by dressing in clothes of the opposite sex and frequently masturbates or has intercourse in this condition. The transsexual merely regards himself as correctly dressed when he appears in women's clothes and therefore does not necessarily feel sexually aroused.

The cause of these conditions is very obscure. Transsexualism could well come about by the same hormonal mechanism suggested for exclusive homosexuality, i.e. non-masculinisation of the female brain centre in a morphological male, or vice versa (masculinisation of a morphological female). But the question remains unanswered as to why some homosexuals should continue to regard themselves as males with an abnormal orientation while others should desire to be thought of as females and strive to change their bodily appearance so that behaviour and morphology are consistent. No doubt there are certain life experiences that are capable of affecting a person's gender identity given that he has some kind of contradiction implicit in his biological drives and physical appearance. At the moment we do not know what the critical experiences are.

Other variations

A great many other unconventional choices of sex object and sexual activity, commonly labelled perversions, are available. Some of the best recognised and most popular of these are listed in the table below. It is beyond the scope of this book to examine them each in detail but we may briefly outline a few principles that apply quite broadly. The first is that most of them are almost uniquely male sources of amusement. Women are believed to have fantasies that cover some of these areas but they very seldom come to the attention of the law enforcement agencies as a result of active involvement.

Some classified perversions

Perversion	Basis of arousal
Fetishism	Nonhuman objects, e.g. shoes, stockings, leather or particular aspects of the body such as ankles or knees
Bestiality	Intercourse with animals; masturbating animals
Exhibitionism	Exposure of genitals to an unwilling viewer
Voyeurism	Peeping at other people undressing or having sex
Incest	Sexual relationship with a close family member, e.g. daughter, sister
Rape	Sexual assault on an unwilling adult
Paedophilia	Sexual contact with children
Sadism	Inflicting pain on another person
Masochism	Having pain inflicted upon oneself
Urolagnia	Urinating on another person or being urinated upon
Frotteurism	Rubbing the genitals on other people in a crowd

Selective lodging of complaints might partly account for this (it has been remarked that a man peeping at a nude woman is a voyeur but a woman looking at a naked man is watching an exhibitionist) but there is definitely more to it than that. Many of these perversions, e.g. rape, bestiality, incest and frotteurism can be seen as extensions of sexual interest to situations that have some resemblance to the appropriate sex object (a willing adult female) but which have been defined by society as taboo. Since men have a higher sex drive, higher aggression and a greater predisposition to anti-social behaviour in general, it follows that they are much more likely to engage in perverted sexual activity. As we have said, the stronger the libido, the further it is bound to generalise around the prime target preset by the foetal hormones.

This is not a complete explanation, however, for many of the perversions in our list have the characteristics of a compulsion. That is, the individual becomes fixated on his particular 'thing' and it becomes almost his sole source of sexual pleasure. He finds that he just *has* to do it and there is no other way that he can achieve arousal or orgasm. Psychoanalysts have produced many convoluted explanations for this behaviour which modern psychologists have not found very illuminating; the two factors most often cited today are neurological damage and accidental conditioning experiences occurring to a susceptible personality.

There is some evidence that fetishism in particular is related in some way with epileptic seizures. Lesions in the temporal lobe of the brain occurring early in the life of the individual have often been found to be associated with sexual deviations of a fetishistic nature. It seems probable that a significant proportion of cases of fetishism, transvestism, and some of the other deviations are associated with subtle brain injuries occurring around the time of birth or within the first two years of life. However, the lesion probably plays a predisposing role rather than making the behaviour inevitable.

Evidence for the role of conditioning comes from a study by S. J. Rachman in which boot fetishes were produced in five volunteer subjects by showing them a series of sexually arousing pictures immediately preceded by slides of footwear. The presence of the fetish was established by showing that the boot pictures alone had acquired the capacity to evoke sexual arousal. After this, the subjects were all 'cured' again – despite several protestations.

It seems that some part of a sexual deviation is due to positive motivation that is excessive or misplaced. Some contribution is added by learning processes such as accidental associations between sexual arousal and stimuli that occur in association with them. Another factor that is no doubt involved in some cases is a learned fear of appropriate sex objects. The tendency for some deviations such as incest and paedophilia to occur with highly religious and moralistic persons might be explained in terms of the strength of prohibitions against normal sex, in the same way that fear of women has sometimes been implicated in the origins of homosexuality. Acquired fears tell us why a person does not engage in regular, socially acceptable sexual activity, but of course it does not tell us why one individual chooses masturbation as his preferred alternative, another adopts homosexuality and still others prefer voyeurism, exhibitionism or paedophilia. The previous explanations are necessary to account for the idiosyncratic nature of perversions.

Whatever the causes of these variations we should be tolerant of them up until the point where the freedom of other people is jeopardised. Homosexuality appears to be natural for a statistical minority of the population and when practised between willing partners is a harmless mode of sexual expression. The same usually applies to fetishism and mild degrees of sadism and masochism. The public has a right to be protected, however, from rapists, paedophiliacs, frotteurs and the like, who take their pleasure at the expense and embarrassment of other people, regardless of whether their behaviour is classified as criminal or sick.

7

Inadequate lovers

According to Desmond Morris, humans are unusual apes in that they form long-term attachments, or pair-bonds, reminiscent of certain species of birds. He connects this evolutionary embellishment with certain other uniquely human characteristics. One is the amount of pre-copulatory foreplay that we indulge in — all of the kissing, cuddling, caressing, and other activities which bring sexual excitement up to a high pitch before the consummation. Whereas the sequence of copulation in monkeys is usually over within a matter of seconds, humans engage in an elaborate ritual which averages half an hour. Ideally this results in orgasm for both partners, which is highly rewarding and serves to reinforce the partnership. In other primates females do not experience orgasm at all; in humans the female orgasm is elusive, requiring a certain amount of time and patience, as well as optimal physical and psychological conditions. Another unique characteristic of the human female is her receptiveness throughout the cycle, even at times when she is not fertile. Morris believes that this evolutionary development has also occurred to support the double function of human intercourse: not only does it serve the purpose of reproduction, but also the fertilisation of a love-bond between the couple.

If that be so, then, what happens if the sexual contact is unsatisfactory or ceases to be rewarding for some reason? We would expect the love-bond to break down progressively and the partners eventually to separate. Indeed, that is precisely what happens. It is impossible to estimate how many broken marriages are attributable to dissatisfactions in the area of sex or the number of people who remain unhappy isolates as a result of some sexual disability or incompetence. Probably the numbers in each case are astronomical, for the more the taboos on discussing sexual problems are lifted, the more we see emerging from the closet. Three problems in particular have proved to be particularly common and debilitating — premature ejaculation, impotence and frigidity. The work of Masters and

Johnson and others on the nature of the human sexual response, and the factors which disrupt it, has led the way to effective treatments for these disorders, and it is this work that is now outlined.

The sexual response cycle

In 1966 William Masters and Virginia Johnson published their first, very important, book called *Human Sexual Response*. In it they gave a detailed description of what happens physiologically to men and women during the act of sexual intercourse — an authoritative account based on the observation of more than ten thousand orgasms under laboratory conditions. Isolated studies and clinical observations had been available in the scientific literature before that time but the Masters and Johnson work was unique in scope and methodology. Among their novel instruments, for example, was a dildo-shaped camera which could be used to simultaneously excite the female subject and film the changes taking place inside her vagina.

The monitoring of physiological arousal indices such as heart rate, blood pressure, and respiration, revealed a cycle of sexual response that was remarkably similar for masturbation and intercourse, and parallel between men and women. It was analysed into four phases · excitement, plateau, orgasm and resolution.

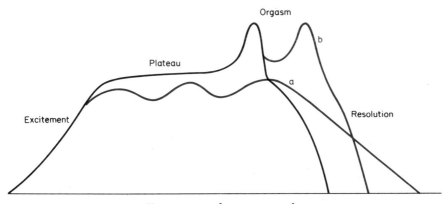

Human sexual response cycles

Sexual response cycles can be graphically represented as above. The solid line is the typical male pattern, which is also quite common in females. The red lines show two fairly common female variants: failure of orgasm (a) and multiple orgasm (b).

1 The *excitement phase* is initiated by any stimulus that is erotic to the individual, be it visual, auditory, tactile or imaginal. There is engorgement of the tissues in the genital area leading to penis erection in the male and vaginal lubrication in the female. In addition there is erection of the nipples in the female (and some males), swelling of the breasts, and certain changes in the clitoris and labia.

2 In the *plateau phase* the man's testicles increase in size by about 50 per cent and are pulled high up into the scrotum. In the woman, there is a swelling of the outer part of the vagina which reduces its circumference and tightens its grip on the penis, while the inner part of the vagina and the uterus become more cavernous. The clitoris is shortened in length and retracts away from the possibility of direct friction with the penis. All of these changes basically reflect increases in blood supply and muscular tension around the genital area.

3 The *orgasm* is the brief few seconds of peak excitement during which all voluntary control is lost. In the woman there are rhythmic contractions of the outer part of the vagina, the uterus, and sometimes also the anal sphincter muscles. Contrary to early beliefs the uterine contractions do not operate to suck seminal fluid in through the cervical opening; the contractions actually proceed downwards from the upper end to the cervical end, like those occurring in child labour.

The male orgasm is similar in that it consists of a series of rhythmic contractions of the penis timed at the same intervals as those of the vagina; these propel the seminal fluid through the urethra under considerable pressure so that in orthodox coitus it is deposited around the area of the cervix at the inner end of the vagina.

In both men and women, these events are accompanied by numerous other bodily changes. Heart rate increases to up to 180 beats per minute, respiration also races, and blood pressure is raised. Much of the skin is covered in a flush and there are strong contractions of the muscles in the neck, arms, legs, back and buttocks. The face is often contorted into a grimace and the woman in particular is likely to emit vocal noises.

4 The *resolution phase* is a return to the unstimulated status quo. It occurs relatively quickly if orgasm has been achieved and is experienced as a feeling of great release and tranquillity. Women are capable of having another orgasm during this period if effective stimulation is resumed; men have a definite refractory period during which restimulation is impossible, its length varying according to age, fitness, extent of deprivation, novelty and desirability of the partner.

There is one physiological change during the resolution period which might affect the chances of pregnancy occurring. Recent work by Dr Cyril Fox in London, using radio-telemetry devices implanted in the uterus, has revealed a marked drop in uterine pressure immediately following female orgasm. This pressure drop seems sufficient to assist in the process of sperm transport from the vagina into the uterus. In other words, female orgasm might well enhance the chances of conception but the sucking action of the uterus, which

Masters and Johnson proved did not occur during orgasm itself, appears to operate after the climax, during so-called resolution.

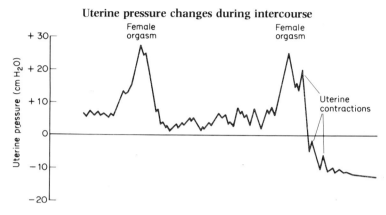

Uterine pressure changes during intercourse

Dr Cyril Fox of St Bartholomew's Hospital, London, has used a radio pill to monitor pressure changes inside the uterus during sexual intercourse. The above is a typical record taken during a single occasion of intercouse. Consistent with the work of Masters and Johnson, the uterine contractions during orgasm increase the pressure inside the uterus rather than providing an insuck action. There is, however, a distinct decrease in uterine pressure during the resolution phase which could assist the passage of sperm through the cervix.

Some myths exploded

Apart from describing the sequence of physiological events that take place during intercourse and masturbation, Masters and Johnson were also able to provide firm evidence in relation to certain highly controversial points about human sexuality.

One of their most important findings concerns the role of the clitoris in female orgasms. Before the St Louis research it was widely believed that women could experience two different kinds of orgasm, one resulting from stimulation of the clitoris and the other derived from friction on the inside of the vagina. Masters and Johnson, however, showed that clitoral and vaginal orgasms were physiologically indistinguishable. Apparently, all of women's orgasms are mediated or triggered by the clitoris, their highly sensitive penis analogue, but *indirect* stimulation of the clitoris is preferable to a direct attack. Orgasm is not ideally produced by direct contact between penis and clitoris but by rhythmic movement of the clitoral hood across the top of the clitoris. This, in fact, is what occurs during normal intercourse since the clitoral hood is an extension of the labia and therefore participates in the movements produced by the thrusting penis. It is consistent that very few women masturbate by directly rubbing the clitoral glans; they usually find an area close to it where they can simulate the movements that occur during intercourse. This information has proved very useful in marriage guidance and sex therapy.

Some other interesting findings were as follows:

1 Orgasms produced by masturbation seemed to be just as intense, and often more so than, orgasms obtained during intercourse.

2 The size of a man's penis was not a significant factor in the enjoyment obtained by him or his partner. The vagina expands just sufficiently to accommodate the penis and produce the same degree of friction whatever its size. In any case, erect penises vary in size much less than flaccid ones, i.e. penises that are small when limp increase their size disproportionately to erection.

3 Circumcision makes no appreciable difference to the sexual response of either the man or the woman.

4 Women are quite able to enjoy intercourse during menstruation, particularly during the second half of the period. They also desire sex during the second trimester of pregnancy just as much as when they are not pregnant and intercourse during this time does not generally appear harmful to either mother or foetus.

Sexual inadequacy and its causes
The cycle of sexual response described above only holds true if everything is running smoothly. One could say it applies to normal people, except that the number of couples who encounter difficulty at some time in their relationship is quite staggering. The major types of sexual dysfunction are as follows:

Primary impotence The man has never been able to achieve erection adequate for penetration.

Secondary impotence The man is at present unable to achieve erection though he has been successful in the past.

Situational impotence The man is impotent under certain circumstances, e.g. is able to make love to his mistresses but not his wife.

Premature ejaculation The man is unable to control ejaculation long enough for his partner to achieve orgasm on a reasonable proportion of occasions. In some cases ejaculation occurs before entry or even before erection.

Ejaculatory incompetence A rare disability in which the man is able to erect and enter but cannot ejaculate.

Dyspareunia Intercourse is painful in some way for one or other of the partners — more often the woman.

Primary orgasmic dysfunction The woman has never experienced orgasm either from intercourse or masturbation.

Situational orgasmic dysfunction The woman is unable to have orgasms in certain situations. E.g. she may climax easily on holiday but not at home.

Vaginismus Involuntary contractions of the outer part of the vaginal canal make insertion impossible.

In pursuing the causes of these sexual problems, Masters and Johnson very soon arrived at the conclusion that they were more often psychological than physiological. Physical examination of their patients seldom turned up any anatomical or physiological source of the malfunction. The fact that a man may be impotent with his wife but not with his mistress, or that a woman may be orgasmic on holiday but not at home, is convincing evidence for the importance of psychological factors. Certain diseases such as urethritis or multiple sclerosis and temporary physiological states such as tiredness, excessive intake of alcohol, or other drugs, were occasionally found to be involved, but in the vast majority of cases the dysfunction could be traced to some inhibitory attitude towards the partner or sex in general.

Masters and Johnson assumed that a variety of background factors could be responsible for sexual disorders — a strict religious upbringing, unpleasant early experiences, homosexual inclinations, misinformation, and so on. In this respect they are in agreement with Freudian theory. However, when it comes to treatment of these problems Masters and Johnson adopt a direct, behaviourally orientated approach which concentrates on the bad habits and attitudes that are maintaining the problem in the here and now. Their clinical impression is that the attitudes most detrimental to sexual fulfilment are anxiety about one's performance and the tendency for some people to 'stand aside' mentally and adopt a spectator role. The nature of these problems may be clarified by two examples.

A fairly common type of female orgasmic dysfunction (frigidity) is represented by the woman who is afraid of losing control. As she feels excitement rising towards the point of orgasm she reacts to it as a threat and takes mental and physical measures to 'turn herself off' again. She experiences inhibitory emotions such as guilt and anxiety and may unconsciously adjust her physical position in such a way as to reduce the stimulation that threatens to bring her to orgasm. It has been estimated that about 10 per cent of women never experience orgasm, and although incompetence in their male partners is often implicated, self-defeating attitudes of the kind described are the most common causes.

A second common example is the man who has a history of reliable erection but one day finds that he is unable to get an erection for one reason or another — perhaps he is just tired, or has had too much to drink, or is sickening for the flu. He is caught entirely by surprise and becomes anxious and fearful that age is catching up with him or that something has gone irreparably wrong with his equipment. On the next occasion of love-making he is terrified that the same thing is going to happen again — and it does, as a kind of self-fulfilling prophecy. His sexual arousal is inhibited by that very anxiety. It is easy to see how a vicious circle of apprehension and performance failure can be built up, leading to a condition of chronic impotence.

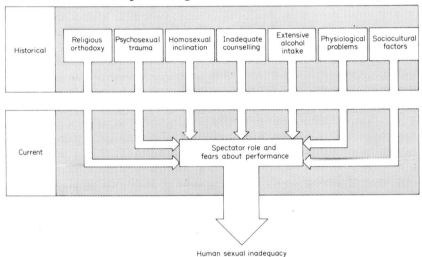

Human sexual inadequacy

The causes of sexual inadequacy

Masters and Johnson believe that a great many different factors in a person's background may contribute towards sexual inadequacy, but in therapy they concentrate on modifying current attitudes and behaviour. Most of the sexual disorders are maintained in the here and now because one or both of the partners assume a spectator role and are apprehensive about their performance.

Treatment techniques

As we have said, when it comes to therapy the historical origins of sexual disorders are very largely irrelevant. What is needed is some kind of retraining or attitude modification procedure which can be applied to the problem as it is currently manifested. Some of the techniques mostly commonly used by Masters and Johnson and other sex therapists will now be described. Most of these have evolved through clinical experience of what is effective, including follow-up studies of their patients for up to five years after treatment.

A basic assumption that pervades much of the work of Masters and Johnson is that sexual enjoyment will follow fairly naturally if anxiety and self-consciousness do not interfere. So therapy is aimed at reducing or removing fears of performance and freeing the couple from any tendency to assume a spectator role during sexual activity.

In the classical Masters and Johnson approach, couples are booked into a luxurious hotel so that they are removed from everyday cares and stresses. Over a two-week period they meet with a male and female therapist each day – the situation described as a 'therapeutic foursome'. The idea is that on some matters the wife may be able to communicate better with a female therapist and the husband will have better rapport with a male therapist. Sometimes the reverse is the case, but at least there is a reduced chance of one of the partners getting the feeling that the therapist is taking sides. Equally it is important that both members of the partnership are seen conjointly, even though they themselves may believe that only one partner is responsible for the problem. Masters and Johnson insist that there is no such thing as an uninvolved partner in a marriage relationship. Some patients, of course, have individual sexual problems but no permanent partner (indeed they may find it impossible to keep a partner because of their problem). In such cases it is necessary to provide a slightly different kind of therapy, in which the patient is advised how to behave when a prospective partner becomes available.

Treatments prescribed for impotence and female orgasmic dysfunction (frigidity) have a great deal in common. The prescription is aimed at slowing down the love-making sequence to give time for things to happen, while at the same time eliminating fears of performance. This is achieved by instructing the couple to take turns at caressing each other over a period of several nights during which time intercourse and orgasm are expressly forbidden. This teasing procedure, which involves no pressure to perform, is frequently found to restore male potency to the extent that the abstinence rule is broken well before it is officially due to terminate. 'Non-demand pleasuring', as it is called, has also proved very effective in the treatment of frigidity problems in that the female partner is, perhaps for the first time, given time and freedom to experience pleasure for herself.

An auxiliary technique that has been found very useful in connection with female orgasmic difficulties was described several decades ago by Dr Helena Wright. The man's hand is placed over the woman's mons or vulva. She places her hand over the top of his and guides its movements in ways she finds erotically arousing. This has a number of potentially beneficial effects. It may satisfy the need of some women to take the lead in the love-making, and the fear of 'losing control' may be reduced by the fact that she remains in actual control of the arousal process. It also serves to teach the man what kind of movements, degree of pressure, speed of rhythm and so on she finds most pleasurable, so that he can know better how to arouse her himself later on. In fact, it amounts to a combination of self-masturbation and heterosexual contact, partaking of each in a unique way that sometimes produces valuable spin-off in terms of insights and experience.

Another technique that is often recommended for female orgasmic dysfunction employs the 'female superior' position of intercourse. The man lies on his back passively while the woman sits on top of him and gently inserts his penis. Her instruction is to treat it like a toy and attend to the pleasurable sensations that it provides. Again, the emphasis on containment without frantic thrusting helps the couple to slow down the sequence sufficiently for the woman to obtain some personal satisfaction. Note, this procedure highlights the fact that it is often an arbitrary matter as to whether the couple's problem is defined as frigidity or premature ejaculation. Is the woman too slow or the man too fast? The very assignment of blame by the partners themselves may have further impaired their intimacy; the therapists must be careful not to make the same mistake.

The procedure that is used in the correction of premature ejaculation (where this definition of the problem is inescapable) is called the Semans technique, after Dr James Semans of Duke University Medical School, who first described it in 1955. It is based on the ability of men to recognise the sensation that occurs shortly before ejaculation becomes inevitable — the point of no return. The penis is stimulated until the warning feeling is experienced and then stopped abruptly, perhaps by squeezing the shaft of the penis until excitement subsides. After a rest period of ten minutes or so, this procedure is repeated. This exercise is repeated three or four times a night for several days and has proved to be an effective treatment for premature ejaculation in the vast majority of cases. It is not clear exactly how it works. Perhaps a conditioned feedback circuit is set up by which the critical pre-orgasmic point of excitement is associated with inhibition (derived from the squeeze experience) and this causes an automatic cut-back in the level of excitement just in time to prevent ejaculation. Alternatively, it may be that the individual learns to bring his genital reactions under voluntary control by paying attention to the sensations that accompany their activity. Either way, it could be viewed as a process of learning what the frigid female has to unlearn in order to overcome her problem. The squeeze technique can be practised alone, or preferably by the wife, who at the same time can learn to recognise the point of no return so that in intercourse itself she can stop moving in time to allow his excitement to subside and thus help to delay his orgasm.

In recent years, a great many other centres for sex research and therapy have opened up around the world in response to an apparently newly discovered need, and many new techniques have been added to the battery pioneered by Masters and Johnson. One supplementary approach to the treatment of impotence in particular, and to some extent frigidity also, is that of trying to top up a suspected deficit in libido. Most of the earlier therapists had assumed that the major causes of sexual inadequacy were inhibitory in nature, i.e. that the sex drive would be high enough for the job if only it were not held back by 'hang-ups' of various descriptions. The alternative interpretation that seems valid and useful in some cases at least is that libido may be too low. Apparently, some people simply do not have sufficient interest in sex to enable them to become aroused and perform when they would like to. Inevitably, they or their partner end up being dissatisfied or frustrated. This being the case, some therapists have considered various techniques for raising sexual libido.

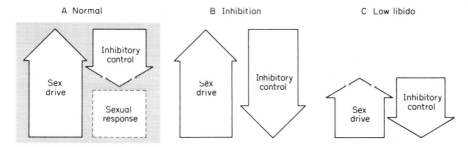

Two models of psychological impotence and frigidity
In the sexually healthy person (A) a certain degree of sexual responsiveness is possible because inhibitions are not so strong as to nullify sex drive completely. Some forms of sexual inadequacy arise because fears and anxieties are so strong that they offset a sex drive of normal intensity (B). Other cases of impotence and frigidity result from simple insufficiency of libido (C). Clearly, different kinds of treatment are indicated for these two forms of sexual inadequacy. A third form of sexual inadequacy (not represented here) is that due to organic or physiological disease.

We have seen in chapter 5 that no satisfactory aphrodisiacs have yet been developed which would enable us conveniently to modify a person's drive from the inside by chemical means. Injection of testosterone is sometimes used but has distinct disadvantages – it may even turn off the individual's own supply of that hormone. This leaves us with the option of modifying the erotic arousal value of the environment. Some therapists, such as Dr Patricia Gillan, a sex therapist practising in London, have experimented with the therapeutic use of visual and auditory erotic stimuli – pornography in other words. Positive results have been obtained with this method in selected cases of impotence and frigidity, sometimes in combination with anxiety-reduction techniques. A certain proportion of middle-aged patients and patients with weak libidos appear rejuvenated and revitalised after treatment of this kind.

Again, the theoretical basis of the improvement is unclear. There may be a direct physiological effect on the sex organs mediated through the hypothalamus and endocrine system, e.g. via the release of testosterone into the blood stream. Or the viewing of pornography might operate to change attitudes and reduce anxiety via a kind of modelling effect. ('If other people can do all this in front of the lights and cameras, then it must surely be all right for us to do it in private.')

Another recent innovation in therapy for impotence and frigidity is the mechanical stimulator. The idea is that if a woman who has never experienced orgasm before can have one induced with a vibrator, she may be better placed to recognise and focus upon relevant preliminary sensations during intercourse. Similarly, electrical stimulators have been used to restore confidence in some cases of male impotence.

Sexual performance and love
Some readers might think it strange that we have included a chapter on sexual responsivity in a book about attraction and love. No doubt, some would be inclined to object that true love is not identical with sexual capacities. Indeed, that is so — 'Love feeds on many kinds of food.' But it has a particular appetite for mutually rewarding sexual experiences. Both Desmond Morris and Masters and Johnson in their latest book, *The Pleasure Bond*, have emphasised the importance of mutual sexual satisfaction in the development and maintenance of the love-bond. If the sexual relationship breaks down, the love feelings are frequently soon to follow. This was the justification of Masters and Johnson for undertaking their studies of human sexuality — it is also a justification for reviewing their work here.

It took a great deal of courage and resolution on the part of William Masters and Virginia Johnson to confront the taboos and lay their reputations on the line in pursuing this area of research. But their work has paid off admirably in terms of the alleviation of human suffering and despondency. Around 80 to 90 per cent of the sexual problems that are now coming to light with increasing frequency are responsive to some combination of the techniques we have described — techniques that we owe to a great extent to the pioneering investigations of Drs Masters and Johnson. By unveiling some of the darkest mysteries of love, Masters and Johnson and their followers have contributed to the preservation of a great deal of love that would otherwise have perished insidiously.

8

The novelty factor

Beauty is all very well, but who ever looks at it when
it has been in the house three days?

G. B. Shaw

What happens if two healthy, adult rats, one male and one female,
are confined together in a cage? One piece of behaviour that will
almost certainly be observed is copulation — initially at a fairly high
rate of repetition. After the honeymoon, though, there is a distinct
decline in the amount of sexual activity that takes place; as the couple
become familiar with each other sexual interest seems to fade. Now
if the female is removed and replaced by another, the full interest and
vigour of the male is restored and the rate of coitus immediately
elevated to the earlier high level. This dependence of libido in rats on
having new partners has been referred to as the 'Columbus effect'.

The Columbus effect is not restricted to rats. It is equally apparent
with primates. For example, in one study, eleven Macaque monkeys,
previously strangers to each other, were observed in the process of
group formation. Sexual behaviour was fifteen times more frequent
during the initial period of encounter than in any subsequent period.
Some of the early enthusiasm may have been socially motivated
rather than purely sexual, but the novelty of the sexual liaisons was
no doubt a major stimulus.

An unmistakably parallel phenomenon also occurs with human
partnerships. Married couples have a great deal of intercourse during
the first year of marriage after which there is typically a dramatic
fall-off. They then settle into a low and gradually declining rate. The
slow decline could be due to ageing, but the sharp decline is probably
due to loss of novelty since a very high rate of intercourse may be
re-achieved with a mistress or lover.

Sexual boredom is one of the strongest factors operating against
stable mateships in humans as well as other animals. Although
seldom cited in the divorce courts because it is not considered a
legitimate excuse for disbanding a marriage, it is probably at the root

of most marital breakdowns. Furthermore, there is very little that can be done about it. This is one sexual problem that Masters and Johnson and other sex therapists have no real answer to. They can suggest varying the positions of intercourse, the room in which it is had and so on. But even swinging upside down from the chandelier the battle is eventually lost.

Because the need for novelty is basic to an understanding of promiscuity, infidelity, polygamy, 'swinging' and a good many 'perversions', we round out the picture of human love and sexual behaviour by devoting this chapter to it. In addition, we discuss individual differences in sexual appetite and curiosity, and the personality and other factors that determine them.

Why the need for novelty?
Since the search for novelty seems to make for discontentment and get us into nothing but trouble, the first question that arises is that of its motivational source. Unfortunately no easy answer is available. The thirst for new sexual experiences seems to be one aspect of a general need for novelty and freshness that is built into our biological nature. As we go up the evolutionary scale through mammals and primates there is an increasing exploratory drive. Rats will explore mazes for the sake of curiosity alone, even when they are hungry and know from past experience which alleys will lead them to food. Monkeys will expend considerable effort to obtain the reward of looking at something new to them, and the curiosity of man is exemplified by his intrepid exploration of unknown continents and, recently, space. A desire for novel experiences of all kinds seems to be an innate characteristic of all higher animals, and especially man.

The drive towards sensation and excitement does not go entirely unopposed. In all species and individuals it is balanced by a directly opposite need — that for security. While all people have some urge towards both excitement and security, there are differences between individuals and differences between men and women in the relative importance of these two needs. On average, extraverts have a greater need for excitement and variety than introverts, and men are more sensation-seeking than women. The evolutionary significance in variation along the security—exploration dimension is clear. It is important for a species to have some individuals who take risks in order to extend the territorial and other frontiers of the social group, just as it is important to have others who are careful, conservative, and home-loving so as to preserve the line in case the more curious are eliminated. The sex differences in this area probably arose out of the differentiation of labour — males moving about geographically for hunting and food-gathering, while females stay close to the nest to nurture the young. We shall return to these differences later.

Referring specifically to the lust for sexual novelty, it is possible to point to other possible evolutionary functions. One male is capable of impregnating many females, so his fertility and virility might be somewhat wasted if he bonds himself exclusively to one female (especially if females outnumber males in the group). If a female is constantly faithful to one male who happens to be infertile for any reason, then her reproductive capacity is also wasted. A certain amount of flexibility in contacts prevents these occurrences. Variety in sexual liaisons might also help the species by mixing genes to a greater extent. Variation in genetic mixes is fundamental to the process of natural selection. This is partly why all human societies have adopted incest taboos of one sort or another, and the restriction on incest might actually be bolstered with a drive towards novel, anonymous sex.

Monogamy and its alternatives

Religious leaders and other conservative elements in society would have us believe that monogamy is a natural order for mankind. Yet an examination of sexual partnerships in animals and other cultures reveals that monogamy is in fact very rare. Most primates tend towards polygyny, i.e. one male having several female mates. By simple arithmetical deduction this means that other males must go without, and this is frequently the case. The monkey troop usually contains several 'bachelors' who may hope to displace the dominant male who owns the harem at some time but in the meantime have to make do with the occasional stolen liaison with one of his wives while his back is turned.

Similarly with humans, the most common pattern of mateship is a multiple one in which two or more females are attached to one male. Our own society is one of a very small minority of cultures (16 per cent is the figure given in one survey) which restrict sexual liaisons to single mateships. In one or two very exceptional human societies both men and women are permitted to enter multiple mateships, but even when the cultural norms permit, women seldom do actually establish polyandrous relationships. If any state of affairs is natural, then, it is polygyny − a moral code that allows men to have as many wives as they are capable of winning and economically supporting.

Where a society, such as our own, professes standards that differ from the overall human norm, it is worth looking in closer detail to see to what extent the behaviour of its individual members really corresponds to the official code. Theoretically no form of sexual encounter outside of marriage is acceptable in Western society, yet there is no doubt that a lot do occur. Surveys show that around

50 per cent of men have extramarital relations at some time in their lives, and about 25 per cent of women. It is also known that a higher proportion of each sex feel inclined towards having an affair but are restrained from doing so for some reason, and that the proportion of people having (or admitting to) affairs has been steadily increasing over the last few decades. The main limiting factor for men is opportunity; for women it is social pressure and moral compunction. Kinsey maintained that 'the human male would be promiscuous throughout the whole of his life if there were no social restrictions'. This is probably an exaggeration, but it does seem that the majority of men have a desire for variety in their partners, and so do quite a lot of women.

Western society offers a number of partly legitimised outlets for the novelty drive. The most common of these is the extramarital affair which is usually conducted without the knowledge of the spouse, though it is likely to be discovered or confessed later. Some couples feel that deception is worse than jealousy, so they enter an agreement to tell each other about their extramarital affairs. An elaboration of this is mate-swapping or 'swinging' in which connivance may be taken to the extent of vicarious enjoyment of each other's extramarital experiences and jealousies are suppressed in favour of group feelings. Another recognised safety valve which is still illegal in many countries is prostitution. The most drastic solution to the novelty problem is divorce. Many sociologists have pointed out that the other outlets may actually support the institution of marriage rather than undermine it. Certainly it seems significant that affairs and prostitution have always been well tolerated in catholic countries which forbid divorce.

The double standard
Most societies, including our own, put more severe restrictions on the sexual behaviour of females than males. Though conscious attempts have recently been made to counter this discrimination, virginity and chastity are still regarded as more important for women than men. What are the origins of this double standard? One possibility is that men, being physically stronger and socially dominant, have arranged the rules in their own favour. The weakness of this notion is that since females are necessary for sexual pleasure it would have been a great deal more advantageous for the men to set permissive rules for women as well as themselves.

A more likely explanation is that because the female stands to get pregnant as a result of a sexual encounter, she has more reason to be cautious. We would expect women to require love as a prerequisite to intercourse because they would be concerned about provision for any offspring that might result. Similarly, men would watch their wives carefully because they would not want to be held economically and otherwise responsible for other men's children. It is perhaps significant that the double standard is beginning to retreat to some extent now that efficient female contraception is available.

Another related basis for the double standard might be the temperamental differences between men and women. As we have noted, there are evolutionary reasons to think that men are adventure-seeking animals, while women put greater stress on nurturance and security. Assuming that men have a greater biological need for novelty, some allowance for this might have been built into the social code. That is, the moralists may have partly given up on men from the start.

In an earlier chapter we implied that men have a higher sex drive than women and that this is determined by their biology. We can now clarify what was meant by that. What men actually have is a greater need for novelty than women; there is no evidence that they have a greater need for sex *per se*. If anything, the reverse may be the case. Once a couple have established some kind of a love bond the man's sexual requirements within the relationship frequently drop off faster than the woman's. At some point the wife may discover that she is initiating a greater amount of sexual activity than her husband. The man, however, is more likely to retain his sexual interest in other people, and this is probably the main sense in which he has a higher libido than the woman. The difference can be described by saying that women want a lot of sex with the man they love; men want a lot of women.

The emotional differences between males and females are nicely illustrated in a survey by sociologist Michael Schofield of the reasons given by boys and girls for having intercourse the first time. The majority of the boys said they were impelled by sexual desire (46 per cent) whereas the girls were most likely to say they were in love (42 per cent). Motives that could be described as curiosity were much more common in boys (25 per cent) than girls (13 per cent). Although a higher proportion of girls than boys claimed to have been under the influence of drink at the time of their first experience (9 per cent as against 3 per cent) nobody was paid for their compliance and most were quite willing. True to popular belief, the boys are more lustful, predatory, and sensation-seeking; the girls amative and romantic.

Schofield also asked his teenage sample whether they expected to remain faithful after marriage. A much greater proportion of boys (9 per cent) thought that they would have extramarital sex than girls (1 per cent). Similarly, a much higher proportion of boys than girls rejected the institution of marriage or expressed negative attitudes about it. These findings probably reflect the adventurous nature of boys compared to girls rather than conformity to social expectations.

Some typical reasons given for first having intercourse
The boys emerge as predatory, lustful and novelty-seeking; the girls submissive and romantic. (from Schofield 1965)

He wanted to. It wasn't rape or anything. Just that I was in love with him. I still am. It wasn't animal savagery on his part. (girl aged 17)

He kept on telling me that this sort of thing is all right for two people who are in love and plan to get married. I thought about it and agreed. I just sort of thought, 'Well he does love me and he wants to marry me, so why not?' Just like that. (girl aged 18)

I went on holiday to have fun. I wasn't in love with her, or anything. That's why I felt bad afterwards. (boy aged 18)

Because I felt I had to prove to myself once and for all that I could, and perhaps also because I wanted to. (boy aged 19)

I felt like it. I felt I was entitled to it after four months. (boy aged 16)

You just get tired of kissing and that. (boy aged 19)

As regards actual sexual behaviour, Schofield found that girls began dating earlier than boys, had more boy friends and relationships that lasted longer. At more advanced levels of intimacy boys had the greater turnover of partners but girls were more sexually active. Thus the boys were apparently seeking diversity and so had a lot of different partners, while the girls sought security in a more stable kind of relationship. It is noteworthy that the boys were sacrificing some actual sex, in favour of satisfying their novelty drive. Girls seem to have an easier time integrating their needs for love and sex. The apparent statistical discrepancy between the accounts given by boys and girls might be partly explained by the finding of a small contingent of highly promiscuous girls who must have been providing a great deal of the variety for the boys. Of course, a girl with promiscuous inclinations is ideally placed because she is unlikely to be short of opportunities.

Personality predictors of sexual experience
Apart from the differences between the sexes, there are a great many other sources of individual variation in sexual preference and behaviour. In Schofield's study, the life styles of sexually experienced teenagers were compared with those of inexperienced young people. Experienced teenagers tended to have lost interest in and left school earlier, and to have changed jobs more frequently than their virginal counterparts. They spent a great deal of time away from home and were less likely to attend church. The girls in particular were more inclined to dislike their mother. Despite their academic and vocational restlessness, the sexually experienced teenagers were earning higher wages and had more money to spend. Smoking was strikingly

associated with sexual experience, particularly for girls. Practically all of the teenage girls who smoked more than twenty cigarettes a day were experienced sexually, as were half of the boys who smoked this amount. Thus the experienced teenagers (both boys and girls) emerged as more restless, extravert and sensation-seeking in their general pattern of behaviour.

Attitudes that differentiate males from females

Question	Percentage difference
If you were invited to take part in an orgy, would you: (a) accept? (b) refuse?	57*
I like to look at pictures of nudes	53
I like to look at sexy pictures	53
The thought of a sex orgy is disgusting to me	−47
If you were invited to see a 'blue' film, would you: (a) accept? (b) refuse?	43
It is all right to seduce a person who is old enough to know what they are doing	38
I believe in taking my pleasures where I find them	37
If you were offered a highly pornographic book, would you: (a) accept it? (b) refuse it?	36
It doesn't take much to get me excited sexually	35
Buttocks excite me	34
I get excited sexually very easily	33
I think about sex almost every day	32
Seeing a person nude does not interest me	−32
Sex without love ('impersonal sex') is highly unsatisfactory	−31

*Positive number means that the statement is endorsed more frequently by men; negative numbers indicate female preferences

Out of a long sex questionnaire these were the items that most strongly separated men from women. The males have a much greater interest in pornography and other visual stimuli and in impersonal, promiscuous sexual activity. These differences are partly due to the fact that men have a more powerful exploratory drive than women. (from Eysenck 1976)

Hans Eysenck of the London University Institute of Psychiatry studied the relationship between questionnaire-measured personality and sexual behaviour in a large sample of students. The three personality traits measured were extraversion (the tendency to be active, sociable and impulsive), neuroticism (the tendency to be emotionally unstable) and psychoticism (a tendency to be toughminded and antisocial). Sexual preferences were assessed by a questionnaire containing attitude items and questions about characteristic behaviour. The extraverts were found to have experimented sexually a great deal more than introverts; they had sex earlier in life, more often, with more different partners, and in a greater variety of positions. Altogether they came out as having a high libido and a strong urge for novelty. Neurotics also seemed to have a strong interest in sex compared to emotionally stable people, but they experienced a great deal of anxiety and guilt which interfered with their performance and enjoyment. Students who scored high on the psychoticism scale were inclined towards impersonal sex and sensational, perverted (sometimes cruel) activities. Again, these correlations between personality and sexual preferences were fairly consistent for men and women, so that we can say that personality factors cut across the sex differences and need to be considered in addition to them. It seems clear, also, that a major psychological need underlying these differences is the need for novelty; some people are impelled towards sensation and excitement much more strongly than others, and this accounts for a great deal of variability in human sexual behaviour.

The psychological basis of social and political attitudes
Sexual attitudes are part of a constellation of attitudes that reflects the relative strengths of the needs for security and novelty. Conservative people seek safety and stability; liberals seek excitement and change. (from Wilson 1973)

Fear of uncertainty *Source of threat*	General conservatism *Attitudinal manifestation*
Supernatural forces Death The unknown and unpredictable Ambiguity	Superstition Religious dogmatism
Anarchy Social disruption	Right-wing politics
Unfamiliar people Foreign influences Deviant behaviour	Ethnocentrism Militarism Intolerance of minorities
Anomie (i.e. lack of 'roots') Disorganisation Dissent	Authoritarianism Punitiveness
Decisions Loss of control of own feelings and desires	Rigid morality Anti-hedonism Adherence to external authority
Complexity Novelty Innovation	Conventionality Conformity
Technological change Erosion of traditional ideas	Anti-science

A person's social and political attitudes also reflect their personality needs for excitement and security respectively. In *The Psychology of Conservatism* (1973), Glenn Wilson has shown how attitudes in virtually all areas of controversy (sex, race, religion, law and punishment, art, science, etc.) are consistently organised around a general factor called conservatism. This major dimension underlying people's attitudes was found in a number of experimental studies to reflect a generalised mode of response to situations of uncertainty. Conservative people resist scientific progress because they feel threatened in a

Sexual behaviour of unmarried college students

	Males		Females	
	Extraverts (%)	Introverts(%)	Extraverts (%)	Introverts (%)
Masturbation at present	72	86	39	47
Petting	78	57	76	62
Coitus	77	47	71	42
Long precoital sex play	28	21	18	21
Cunnilingus	64	52	69	58
Fellatio	69	53	61	53
More than three different coital positions	26	10	13	12

A questionnaire study was carried out on 6,000 German students. For both men and women, extroversion was associated with a more active and varied sex life. The only exception was masturbation, which may be inversely related to the more sociable outlets. (from Giese and Schmidt 1968)

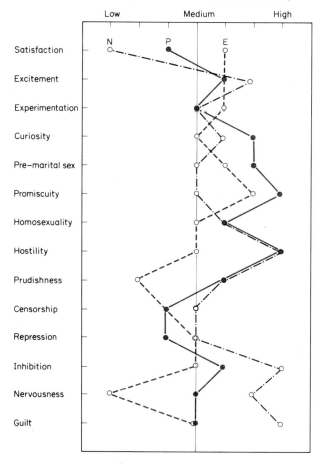

Personality and sexual attitudes
These attitude profiles for extravert, neurotic, and psychotic groups show that E and P are associated with promiscuity and curiosity. (from Eysenck 1976)

changing world; for similar reasons they vote for politicians who are committed to the status quo, go to church, and maintain stable personal relationships. Liberal people value novelty and adventure more than security, and this is why they are sexually permissive, geographically mobile, and favourable towards soft drugs, modern art and supersonic aircraft. Attitudes favourable towards sexual variety are thus part of a general constellation of social attitudes that is based on a high-powered exploratory motive combined with a low degree of susceptibility to fear in situations of uncertainty.

A connection between conservative attitudes and premarital chastity was recently established in a survey by D. R. Thomas at the University of Waikato in New Zealand. He administered the Wilson-Patterson Conservatism Scale to a sample of 337 students along with a questionnaire to assess sexual experience. Those students scoring high on conservatism were much more likely to be virgins than were liberal scorers. This suggests that attitudes determine sexual behaviour to some extent, although it is also possible that some people's attitudes are subsequently modified so as to correspond with, and justify, their previously occurring behaviour. It is interesting that there was a closer tie between conservatism and chastity for women than for men. Perhaps this was because attitudes are a more important limiting factor on the sexual behaviour of women; men are fairly uniformly permissive and limited mainly by opportunity.

Women who have affairs
We have largely answered the question as to which men have extra-marital affairs. Apparently, nearly all of them will given sufficient freedom and opportunity. Women are rather more variable in this respect (whether for social or biological reasons) and it is therefore interesting to look at the factors that predispose them to extramarital sex experience.

	Descriptions of women with varying rates of extramarital sex	%
1	Low marriage rating, like or indifferent to fellatio, low evaluation of marital sex	81
2	High marriage rating, exposure to pornography, have masturbated, like or indifferent to anal intercourse, states other than mountain or prairie region	70
3	High marriage rating, exposure to pornography, have masturbated, dislike anal intercourse, long marriage, initiate sex less than 15 per cent of the time	18
4	Low marriage rating, dislike fellatio, politically conservative	0

The success of a marriage does not always influence whether or not a wife indulges in extramarital affairs. Other factors such as attitudes to sex are also involved.
(from Bell and others 1975)

Robert Bell and colleagues at Temple University in Philadelphia conducted a survey specifically to determine what kind of wife is prone to having affairs. In their sample of 2,262 married women, 26 per cent were found to have had extramarital experience. Of this group, most had had several different lovers, maintaining a series of experiences with each. The average number of occasions on which a woman had sex with each extramarital partner was six times. Bell's evidence indicates, then, that most wives 'don't', but those that 'do' have (or acquire) some taste for it. In other words, there is a kind of dichotomy between faithful and adventurous wives.

As expected, women who rated their marriage as poor were more likely to have engaged in extramarital affairs. However, the fact that some women with good marriages also had affairs suggested that other factors were involved. In particular, women with a liberal life-style as indicated by exposure to pornography, a liking for oral and anal sex, and continued use of masturbation after marriage, were likely to have affairs even if their marriage was successful. Other relevant factors included political orientation and geographical location — women who were politically conservative and who lived in mountain or prairie regions were less likely to have affairs. Some of these factors, such as permissive attitudes and the liking for oral sex, are no doubt partly reflecting variations in the need for novelty. On the other hand, situational factors such as the kind of husband that the woman finds herself married to and geographical differences in social climate are also clearly influential.

The swinging scene

Another mode of response to the problem of sexual boredom that has become increasingly popular in recent years is 'swinging'. Initially this was called wife-swapping, but the term has been dropped because of the sexual inequality and property rights implied. Swinging is a departure from the practice of having affairs in that no deception is entailed. Instead, the partners attempt to confront their jealousy and shake off what they see as repressive inhibitions.

What kinds of people swing?

These are the characteristics of a sample of 503 active mate-swappers in the San Francisco region. (from Smith and Smith 1970)

Age	Range: 15–72; 4% under 21, 7% over 50
	Average: males 34, females 28
Sex	72% male, 28% female
Race	97% white, 2% Negro, 1% 'other'
Marital status	44% married, 32% single, 24% formerly married
Education	52% college graduates, 12% still students, 4% high-school drop-outs
Social class	Generally high
Religion	Background: 50% raised as Protestant, 20% Catholic, 7% Jewish, 23% none or other
	Current affiliation: 16% Protestant, 5% Catholic, 2% Jewish, 77% none or other
Number of sex partners	More than 100 partners: 23% of males, 12% of females
	Median: males 19, females 15

The characteristics of people who swing were studied by James and Lynn Smith from the University of California at Berkeley. They attended over 100 swinging parties in the San Francisco Bay Area, identifying themselves in advance as behavioural scientists making a survey of swinging. Apart from their observations, they administered detailed questionnaires to the participants and obtained responses from 363 men and 140 women. Analysis of these questionnaires revealed that the swingers varied a great deal in age and religious background. A high proportion of them had forsworn all religious affiliation. The majority were well educated and of high social and occupational status.

Swinging was clearly of greater interest to men than women: 72 per cent of the sample were male, and the women that did participate tended to be more discriminating and less active. 23 per cent of the men and 12 per cent of the women reported experience with over a hundred different partners. Only a tiny proportion of women were so devoid of inhibitions that they would joyfully take on all comers until the supply of males ran out, and then only towards the end of the party.

People had many different motives for taking up swinging. Sexual boredom in marriage was commonly cited, but there were many other reasons as well. Some claimed to have done it as a protest against an overly strict upbringing. A puritan upbringing, it seems, can result in a heightened interest in nudity and other aspects of sex – a 'forbidden fruits' reaction. Others took to swinging as a deliberate attempt to shake off their inhibitions or fear of sex. There was no evidence of mental abnormality in the group; the vast majority appeared to be normal, well-adjusted people.

In another study of swingers, by Carolyn Symonds of the University of California at Riverside, two types were distinguished: 'Utopian' swingers and 'recreational' swingers. The Utopian swingers justified their activity on ideological grounds, expressing the belief that love, including its physical expression, is the best counter to social evils such as war, violence, materialism, possessiveness and jealousy. Recreational swingers, on the other hand, 'are simply men and women who believe that it is much more fun for people to have sex together than to play bridge or golf together, and who practice what they believe'.

Whatever the motives or rationale for adopting swinging, many practitioners report psychological benefits. Some reported that their experiences with swinging groups had freed them from their guilt and inhibitions and made them more sexually responsive in general. Married couples frequently reported that swinging had resulted in a restoration of their sexual interest in each other, once the claustrophobic conditions of their relationship had been lifted and outside sexual contacts were also being enjoyed. Other benefits included learning how to handle jealousy and vicarious enjoyment of the pleasure obtained by the partner. Since the powerful novelty factor that we have discussed in this chapter seems to dictate that marriage at best follows a transformation from passionate to companionate love we may find that an increasing number of couples opt for swinging as a method of rediscovering sexual excitement without deception and concealment.

9

The evolution of love

Man (including woman) is an exceptional animal — intelligent, equipped with language, and capable of artistic and scientific achievements far beyond those of other Earthly beasts. He is, nevertheless, an animal. As a kind of ape he has similarities with other apes such as gorillas, chimpanzees and orangutans. At higher levels of generality, man is also a primate, a mammal, a vertebrate, and so on. He shares characteristics with each of these groups in progressively declining degrees. A study of similarities with our animal cousins and ancestors helps us to understand the origins of our own behaviour. The differences are also illuminating, for it is possible to trace their evolutionary development and speculate as to their origins.

In animals we see approximate analogues of ourselves behaving in ways that are little affected by our advanced social development. We are also sufficiently detached from them to observe their behaviour objectively, without so much interference from our own value system.

A similar kind of advantage is conferred by the study of other human groups, particularly 'primitive' cultures, of children even in our own culture, and of adults interacting non-verbally. Watch a man talking to a woman across the room at a cocktail party, out of hearing range — the real nature of their social interaction is often more clearly apparent from their expressions and gestures than from their conversation.

This chapter deals with the origins and development of human attraction and love as revealed through comparison with animal mating patterns, comparison of courtship procedures in different cultures, and observation of the non-verbal communication (body language) of children and adults.

The importance of sexual selection
In *The Descent of Man*, Charles Darwin suggested that many of the

characteristics of human beings as we know them today were selected because possessors of them were particularly successful in reproduction. This included the differences between the sexes in body size, colouration, hair distribution, breast size, and other physical characteristics. Sexual selection in favour of an animal occurs because it is more successful in attracting a mate, or because it is more fertile when it does, or because it takes better care of its offspring. In the more than 100 years that have elapsed since then, biologists have come to believe that Darwin actually understated the importance of this principle relative to other aspects of natural selection such as changing climatic conditions. It now seems that the uniqueness of human beings as they appear today is largely attributable to the process of sexual selection.

Sexual attraction in primates
To understand this, it is useful to look at the sex life of apes and monkeys. As any parent who has taken children to the zoo can witness, the female monkey (e.g. baboon or macaque) signals to the male that she is on heat by presenting a swollen red backside.

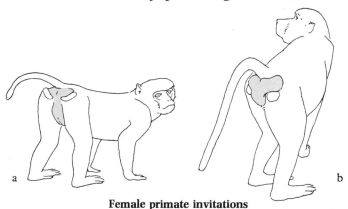

a   b

Female primate invitations
Presentation of a female rhesus monkey (a) and baboon (b). Female invitation signals of this kind evolved in parallel with the importance of vision in primates and are probably the basis of a man's interest in the visual attributes of women.

Typically, she will approach the male of her choice, bend over so as to push her luminous bottom into his face, look over her shoulder and emit friendly, inviting grunts. The chosen male may scrutinise, sniff, and contemplate the prospect for a while, but he will usually proceed to copulate. Females presenting with heat symptoms are clearly preferred by the males and the significance of the visual display (red swellings) appears to have developed in connection with the increasing importance of vision in primates (especially relative to the sense of smell).

For reasons to be discussed, the human parallels of monkey heat-signals are very subtle. Females in certain African tribes show an enlargement of the labia minora, dubbed the 'Hottentot's Skirt' by early explorers. This is a natural anatomical elaboration, appearing in girls at puberty. It does not vary with the menstrual cycle as does the appearance of the 'sexual skin' in monkeys, but it does show a marked change in colour from pink to purple/red during sexual excitement. The attractiveness of this characteristic is suggested by the fact that it is brought about by artificial manipulations by some tribes in whom it does not occur naturally, e.g. Bantus and Basutos.

Human sexual signals?

Extended buttocks of a Hottentot woman (a). A Victorian bustle dress (b). A prominent backside in the human female, whether natural or artificially exaggerated, may represent the sexual swelling of nonhuman primates.

The attractiveness of an extended female backside is suggested by the subcutaneous fat deposits which appear in the buttocks of all women, especially certain African groups who display an exceptional posterior prominence, a condition called steatopygy. Female bottoms are frequently accentuated by pin-up photographers, cartoonists, sculptors and dress fashions. High heeled shoes may have evolved as a fashion for women because they push out the backside and accentuate the movement of the buttocks in walking.

Social effects of sexual gestures

Even in monkeys, sexual behaviour is tied up with social relationships. Monkey troops have a more or less stable dominance hierarchy determined by factors such as strength, competence and popularity. Females generally fall towards the bottom end of the hierarchy but in oestrus (heat) they show more aggression and are likely to rise in the social structure. The increased self-confidence which accompanies their rise in oestrogen also motivates them to cross group boundaries to seduce foreign males and temporarily to leave any children they already have – neither of which they would do at other times. The increased aggressiveness of females on heat leads to the threat of fights with males trying to maintain their social position. This threat is usually thwarted by a mating invitation to the male, who is usually thereby appeased, preferring to make love rather than war.

Presentation is in fact quite frequently employed as a gesture of submission. This non-sexual use of the act may be employed by males, or females not in heat, and it serves to reduce aggression in the individual to whom it is directed. In a similar way, mounting may be used to exhibit social dominance rather than for gratification of the sexual instinct.

Male genital displays also serve aggressive rather than sexual purposes at times. This is seen, for example, when one monkey pushes his erect penis in the face of another, lower-ranked individual. One wonders if there might be some connection here with exhibitionism in men – flashers often seem to be miserable, inferior men, and it may be that in exposing their penis, erect or otherwise, they are trying to 'get one up' on women. Some monkeys, called 'sentinels', will sit at the fringes of the group with thighs splayed to reveal a highly coloured erect penis. The purpose seems to be to mark off the groups' territory and warn approaching intruders.

Sexual pleasure and the love-bond

Many mammals breed in a particular season of the year, e.g. the rutting season in deer. At other times, the males have little interest in sex. The primates have evolved a schedule in which the females' fertility and receptivity goes according to a monthly cycle, whereas the male has a fairly continuous interest in sex. Many biologists believe that this is the basis of social life in primates; it is the males' need for regular sex which keeps the monkey troop together.

Humans, it seems, have taken this idea a step further. The woman, although not fertile for any very extended period, is sexually receptive at nearly all times. There may be minor variation in libido through the cycle (some women have orgasms only during ovulation, others claim to feel sexiest immediately after their period – perhaps as a deprivation effect) but sexual liaisons can and do occur at any time of the month. Since no reproductive advantage can be seen for this evolutionary development, most biologists believe its purpose is to tighten social bonding.

Humans appear to be at the highest point on an evolutionary branch that reduces the quantity of offspring produced and, at the same time, concentrates on the quality of care taken in raising them. The alternatives provided by evolution are to produce thousands of offspring and expect a great deal of wastage or to construct a very limited number of infants and devote full care and attention to them. Most primitive species survive very well with the first system; we have adopted the latter, and our current population problem is testimony to its effectiveness.

If children are to be properly cared for, a stable family unit is necessary. This is the probable reason for the extended season for human sexual liaison – the mutual pleasure that sex provides acts to consolidate a bond between the man and woman which keeps them together long enough for the children to have some chance of survival on their own. Of course, other forms of cooperation, such as the exchange of gifts, complementation of skills and enhancement of status are also important in reinforcing the love bond, but sexual pleasure is a major factor. As Desmond Morris put it, 'We now perform the mating act not so much to fertilise an egg as to fertilise a relationship.'

The hypersexual human

Viewed in this light, many other points of difference between humans and other apes are understandable. Apart from the extended period of sexual responsiveness in the female, there is the absence of body hair. Darwin noted that the erogenous and sexually significant zones of primates are devoid of hair and that females have more exposed flesh than males. Therefore, he suggested that the hairlessness of woman was selected because of its attractiveness to men – this characteristic later generalising in large part to men as well.

Morris has recently expanded this idea in his popular book, *The Naked Ape*, arguing that skin exposure also enhances touch contact, which promotes love. Along with nakedness have developed the soft breasts and rounded contours of the human female, sensitive lips, the large size of the penis compared to other primates, flushing of the skin during sexual intercourse, and vasodilation of lips, nose, ear lobes, nipples and genitals. All these changes appear to be associated with production of high sexual arousal through skin contact.

Humans, then, seem to have evolved an extension of the erogenous areas to virtually the whole of the body. Add to this a long courtship period, a large amount of precopulatory foreplay, the appearance of a female orgasm (however elusive it might be) and it is clear that human beings are justly described as the sexiest animals in creation. Morris and others believe that all this elaboration and embellishment of the human mating process serves the purpose of enhancing the bond between lovers for the benefit of dependent children and social cohesion in general. Since mating usually takes place with a particular individual, there is a natural brake on promiscuity, rivalry and jealousy.

Feminist theories of evolution

Not everyone agrees with the Darwin–Morris account of how we came to lose our body hair and of why women are smoother than men. Right from the start there was opposition from two sources – the Church and women. The Church, as everyone knows, preferred the biblical account of Adam and Eve as the basis for the differentiation between men and women. Feminist movements to this day have resented the suggestion that the form of a woman is in a sense designed for the delectation of men. So women have put up various alternative theories of their own. One of the earliest of such theories was the idea that while hairy men might be descended from apes, women have always been women.

> A Lady fair, of lineage high,
> Was loved by an Ape, in the days gone by.
> The Maid was radiant as the sun,
> The Ape was a most unsightly one –
>   So it would not do –
>   His scheme fell through,
> For the Maid, when his love took formal shape,
>   Expressed such terror
>   At his monstrous error,
> That he stammered an apology and made his 'scape,
> The picture of a disconcerted Ape.
>
> With a view to rise in the social scale,
> He shaved his bristles, and he docked his tail,
> He grew Mustachios, and he took his tub,
> And he paid a guinea to a toilet club –
>   But it would not do,
>   The scheme fell through –
> For the Maid was Beauty's fairest Queen,
>   With golden tresses,
>   Like a real princess's,
> While the Ape, despite his razor keen,
> Was the apiest Ape that ever was seen!
>
> He bought white ties, and he bought dress suits,
> He crammed his feet into bright tight boots –

> And to start in life on a brand-new plan,
> He christened himself Darwinian Man!
>   But it would not do,
>   The scheme fell through —
> For the Maiden fair, whom the monkey craved,
>   Was a radiant Being,
>   With a brain far-seeing —
> While Darwinian Man, though well-behaved,
> At best is only a monkey shaved!

(Lady Psyche's song, from *Princess Ida*, W. S. Gilbert, 1884)

More recently, feminists have supported what is called the *aquatic evolution theory*. This is based on the idea of a differentiation of labour between men and women such that the women foraged for shellfish in shallow coastal waters while their menfolk hunted on land. The loss of hair and increase in subcutaneous fat seen in women is then attributed to its survival value in a watery environment — females are more like dolphins than men. This view of women as amphibious apes appealed to the feminists because it implies that they are adapted to water rather than lecherous male interest. It holds some sway among biologists, and there is certainly agreement that some sex differences reflect a division of labour between men and women. However, the Darwin–Morris theory of hair loss and fat distribution explains a much wider range of observations and is much more widely accepted among scientists who have no political axe to grind.

The principle of mimicry

Evolutionists have long stressed the importance of mimicry as a device which aids survival. For example, a harmless animal may imitate the danger signals emitted by a more lethal species, thus deterring some of its potential enemies. Recently it has been realised that mimicry also occurs across sexes in the same species.

When a male monkey presents himself in female fashion, as an act of submission to a more dominant male, the latter is in a sense tricked into responding to a fake female stimulus. This reduces the amount of fighting amongst the males members of the group, and so serves to promote social cohesion. Without this mechanism the only alternative might be for the weaker individuals to flee, which would certainly not benefit the social unit. The females often find it beneficial to imitate male signals such as mounting and genital displays in order to threaten rivals in their own sex. Thus, there is a tendency throughout the primate world for individuals of each sex to present both encouraging female signals and fear-arousing male ones, though with differing balance. This principle sets limits on the ideal degree of difference in physical form between the sexes, which perhaps helps to explain why men in some cultures shave their face, and why clothing and hairstyle fashions vacillate in terms of how markedly they separate men from women.

Parental instinct releasers

Certain attributes of infants (e.g. large head and eyes relative to the body, chubby cheeks) evoke parental care instincts in adults. These signals are echoed by adults for purposes of mate attraction and enhancement of the love-bond. Some of the signal copies are natural (e.g. large eyes and soft complexion in women), others are achieved artificially (e.g. make-up and shaving).

Another type of within-species mimicry that is probably important in the evolution of love is imitation of the infant. Baby primates emit dependency signals which evoke a protective, nurturant response in adults of both sexes. Females make use of this in attracting males; their softer skin, larger eyes and rounder contours (which they emphasise with make-up and clothing) all evoke a kind of parental affection in men. One wonders if the balding of older men also serves the function of mimicking infant dependency signals.

The genital echo theory

Mimicry also occurs within the body of an individual animal. For example, some reptiles have another 'head' at the tail end in order to deter invasion from the rear. With the evolution of intricate face muscles capable of expressing emotions to other members of the species has come a great deal of face-to-face contact. Some primates even engage in front-to-front intercourse. Also, as the primates evolved an erect (upright) posture, more of their underside was exposed to view. Therefore, some apes have found it advantageous to copy their rear-end welcome signals on the front side. The females, in particular, display an area of exposed pink flesh on the breast which is strikingly reminiscent of the sexual skin on their backside.

Primate genital echoes

Breast echoes of the sexual skin of the female gelada. From left to right: the female backside, female frontside, and male frontside. As the amount of face-to-face contact increased in primates it became advantageous for female signals to be copied on the breast. For the female the probable function is sexual titillation; males mimic female signals to appease aggression.

Here is a probable explanation of the interest men show in women's breasts. If the primary female invitation is the view of her vulva framed by the buttocks (their enlargement in women representing a permanent equivalent of heat-swelling in lower primates) then other parts of her anatomy that are round, fleshy, and arranged in pairs, might serve to echo that signal. The most obvious frontal copy would be the breasts, though other areas such as lips, shoulders and knees would also have some erotic interest in proportion to their diminishing resemblance to the primary signal. The human female is unique among primates in having breasts that are swollen and protuberant even when not producing milk. This, together with the permanently

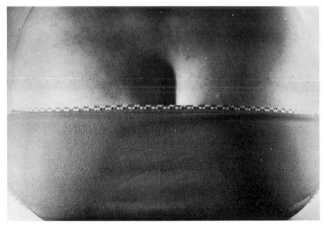

Human genital echoes?

Men are probably attracted by women's breasts because they echo the genital signal. The permanently swollen appearance of both areas evolved in parallel with the extended period of sexual receptivity in the human female.

enlarged bottom, fits well with the evolution of continuous sexual receptivity. In *Intimate Behaviour*, Morris cites an impressive variety of observations which lend credence to the 'genital echo' theory of breast attractiveness. For example, the tendency with women's clothes has been to improve the pseudo-buttock appearance of the breasts by pushing them upwards so they become more round and bulging, and closer together so the cleavage is more like that of the bottom.

The effect of this genital copy on the breast is for men to be constantly 'appeased' and titillated during face to face interaction with women. Fortunately the echoed signal is not so intense as the original, otherwise it is doubtful that civilised society could be maintained. Even so, women in responsible jobs and serious situations are frequently required to dress so as to reduce the intensity of even the secondary signals.

Parent-child intimacy as a basis for adult love
We have dealt with the way in which the sex drive may be harnessed for the social purpose of promoting and stabilising a love bond. Another instinct that contributes greatly to social cohesion, including romantic love, is that relating to brood-care. We noted that girls tend to retain a number of baby-like features into adulthood, that they emphasise them in make-up and clothing, and that men are attracted by them. It is also clear that a lot of basic patterns of parent-child behaviour are carried over into the courting situation. Many of the forms of intimacy indulged in — baby-talk, hand-holding, embracing, kissing, sucking, and biting — are reminiscent of parent-child contact. In fact, a great deal of the behaviour of lovers can be viewed and understood as a return to a parent infant style of tenderness and caring, with the two lovers taking turns in playing the roles of parent and infant.

In monkeys and apes, grooming and lip-smacking are primarily infant-care responses but both have been used as important gestures of greeting and pacification among adults. But again, humans seem to use this instinct for adult social purposes more than any other species. The courtship adaptation of this instinct seems to have evolved parallel with the length of time that infants remain dependent on their parents. Humans remain dependent on their parents virtually right up until the time they are ready for mating, so it is not surprising that the instinct carries over into adolescent and adult courtship behaviour.

Probably it is the addition of various non-sexual motives which characterises romantic love and separates it from purely sexual love. A great many non-sexual motives and interests are no doubt involved (e.g. the exchange of differential skills and property, intelligent conversation, humour, etc.). But among the most important instincts forming the basis of love are the needs for security and protection dating from birth, and the complementary need to offer nurturance to animals that emit dependency signals. It is interesting to observe in passing that, with characteristic stress on the importance of sex, the psychoanalysts have often argued this the other way around. Eibl-Eibesfeldt, in his book *Love and Hate*, notes that 'Sigmund Freud in a strikingly topsy-turvy interpretation, once observed that a mother would certainly be shocked if she realised how she was lavishing sexual behaviour patterns on her child. In this case Freud had got things back to front. A mother looks after her children with the actions of parental care; these she also uses to woo her husband.'

The importance of bodily contact

Primates have an instinctual need for bodily contact, especially when feeling insecure or upset. This is an important part of parent–child intimacy which is carried over into adult love relationships.

The importance of close bodily contact (hugging) to the emotional and sexual development of infant monkeys has been demonstrated in the studies of Wisconsin psychologist Harry Harlow. He deprived infant monkeys of their mothers and provided different kinds of substitute mothers of his own design. Of particular importance was his comparison of artificial mothers that were constructed of wire and provided milk, with those that provided no sustenance but a comfy cloth surface against which to cling. Monkeys reared on the cloth mother developed much more naturally than those reared on the wire mother, thus proving that cuddling is a more important role of the mother than feeding. Monkeys and humans alike seek close bodily contact with another individual when frightened or upset, a behaviour pattern that is present from birth. No doubt the comfort and refuge that is found instinctively in the arms of another person is a major component of adult love.

Kissing, according to some anthropologists, is derived from mouth to mouth feeding with the mother, a procedure that occurs in many primates including some human cultures. Certainly the mouth movements involved bear a close similarity, and lip puckering has become detached from feeding in apes and monkeys to become a ritualised sign of greeting, submission or social interest. Other than this indirect evidence it is difficult to evaluate this theory of the origins of kissing. The connection between the two behaviours is intuitively impressive, but it is very difficult to know at this stage what evolutionary channels have been followed.

Human gestures of invitation

We have described some of the gestures that non-human primates use to signal sexual interest in another member of the species. What gestures do humans commonly employ? Being equipped with speech communication we could be perfectly explicit if we desired. But in fact we very seldom do make outright propositions either verbally or non-verbally. Only at a fairly advanced stage in a relationship do men and women talk openly; in early encounters intentions are conveyed by relatively subtle body movements and facial expressions.

When speech is used it functions more as a kind of 'social grooming' than communication. The actual meaning of what is said tends to be less important than the non-verbal aspects such as inflexion, loudness or softness, pitch, speed of delivery, and so on. When a couple first meet they exchange pleasantries on innocuous subjects and embark on a conversation that neither is really interested in or listening to. They do, however, pay close attention to the 'body language'.

Eye contact is often the first and most significant factor in the display and diagnosis of romantic interest. Men and women can 'make eyes' across a considerable distance and all kinds of mutual understanding can be arrived at on the basis of this alone. The studies of Zick Rubin show that people who are deeply in love with each other, according to their questionnaire responses, engage in a great deal more eye contact than couples who are less in love. Lovers have justly earned the reputation for staring into each other's eyes. Since they are usually past the stage of having to interpret subtle non-verbal cues there must be something rewarding in its own right about eye contact with a loved one.

One aspect of eye signalling which might be more important than we generally realise is pupil size. Studies have shown that our pupils enlarge not only when light dims but also when we are aroused and interested in looking at something. It has been found, also, that people with large pupils are seen as attractive – presumably because their bright, shining eyes signal vivacity and arousal. This might help to explain why people tend to look more romantically interesting in the dark. Not only does low illumination obscure the blemishes in their complexion, it also increases the size of their pupils. If their companion interprets this as romantic interest he or she might reciprocate, thus setting up a feedback system which spirals arousal upwards.

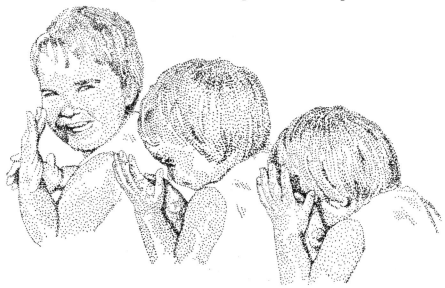

The female modesty ritual
Ritualised hiding (coquetry) is a characteristically female gesture that appears in early childhood (and even in children born blind). In adulthood it may take on a flirtatious significance because it betrays sexual consciousness combined with appropriate modesty (cf. blushing).

Apart from changes in the eyes themselves, a large part of 'making eyes' actually involves movements of the muscles around them. Raising the eyebrows can indicate interest in another person and it is possible to smile with the eyes by screwing them up slightly so that

Warm gestures
Looks into his eyes
Touches his hand
Moves towards him
Smiles frequently
Works her eyes from his head to his toes
Has a happy face
Smiles with mouth open
Grins
Sits directly facing him
Puckers her lips
Nods head affirmatively
Raises her eyebrows
Licks her lips
Uses expressive hand gestures while speaking
Has eyes wide open
Gives fast glances

Non-verbal signals of acceptance and rejection

How a woman tells a man she likes or dislikes him without uttering a word. In a study by Gerald Clore and colleagues at the University of Illinois these behaviours were judged as indicating the greatest amount of warmth and coldness respectively.

Cold gestures
Gives a cold stare
Sneers
Gives a fake yawn
Frowns
Moves away from him
Looks at the ceiling
Picks her teeth
Shakes her head negatively
Cleans her fingernails
Looks away
Chain smokes
Pouts
Picks her hands
Looks around the room
Plays with her split ends
Cracks her fingers

little crease lines form underneath and at the corners. A somewhat flirtatious signal used by girls in particular is the 'modest escape from eye contact'. Parallel with the maidenly blush, a girl who is sexually self-conscious will often register eye-contact then divert her eyes downwards or away. Sometimes this gesture is accompanied by a giggle or by hiding the eyes behind a hand or article of clothing. This behaviour pattern is cross-cultural and occurs very early in childhood. Indeed, its childish association may be part of the basis of its attractiveness in adult women. It suggests purity, submissiveness and embarrassment — all traditional female virtues. Ethologists trace the origins of this gesture to ritual submission and an invitation to chase. (Many women enjoy being chased as a kind of foreplay; this does not mean that they like being raped — what they really want is a display of physical superiority from the man of their choice and perhaps a slight boost in their adrenalin.)

While still on the face, we might note some invitational gestures provided by its second most expressive region, the mouth. A smile is usually accepted as a gesture of greeting and friendship. Ethologists believe that this derives from the 'silent bared teeth face' of primates which is also an appeasing and social expression. It is quite separate from laughing outright, which is normally an expression of aggression and superiority in primates. Pouting, puckering, and tongue-flicking are mouth gestures that have a much more direct invitational quality and are more overtly sexual. Again, it is possible to point to some likely evolutionary origins. Tongue-flicking, for example, could be a ritualised form of licking; in our society it is such a strong signal it is considered slightly indecent — an overt indication of sexuality. The other mouth movements are fairly clearly approximations to the kiss.

There are a number of postural cues that indicate sexual interest. As long ago as 1884 Sir Francis Galton made observations of people seated at dinner parties and concluded that the more attracted they were towards another person the more they leaned towards them. When a man sits next to a woman he finds attractive he will normally, turn his shoulders so as to orient himself towards her. If he crosses his legs, he brings the further leg over the one that is nearer to her, which also has the effect of turning the whole body in her direction. In fact, any kind of physical proximity might signal amorous intent. Usually the man will advance closer to the woman. If she does not feel similarly inclined she signals this by moving back. If she is interested she usually holds her ground or perhaps reciprocates with some approach gesture such as laying her head against his shoulder. Once touch contact is established, its testing, probing functions very soon give way to what the ethologists call 'territory marking' (publicly staking a property claim) and 'grooming' (reassuring and stimulating).

While it is quite usual for men to sit with their legs apart, in many cultures this is regarded as improper for women. The significance of spreading the legs is very clear, even if the genitals are not actually exposed. The rule has been somewhat relaxed with the advent of female trousers but even so the signal is regarded as too strong in normal circumstances. However, if a girl goes too far the other way and squeezes her legs very tightly together she may 'protest too much' and thus make a different kind of comment. As Desmond Morris puts it in *Intimate Behaviour*, 'As with all puritan statements, she reveals that she has sex very much on her mind. In fact, the girl who tries to protect her genitals unduly draws almost as much attention to them as the one who exposes them to view. Similarly, if a skirt rides up slightly when a girl sits down and exposes more leg than she intended, she only enhances the sexuality of the situation by making attempts to tug it down again. The only non-sexual signal is the one that avoids both extremes.'

Who does the selecting?

Male preferences for the females that present the most attractive signals are of major importance in sexual selection, but they are by no means the sole basis. The male dominance hierarchy is also very influential. As an outcome of various encounters male monkeys usually arrive at some agreement as to which has first choice of the females. In some primates the lower order males get paired with low ranked females. Others organise it so that the dominant monkeys may mate with all the females at their most fertile point in the cycle while the lower class males are only permitted coitus at off times in the cycle. Such an ingenious scheme ensures that the successive generations receive a greater genetic contribution from the superior males than from those at the bottom of the hierarchy, the evolutionary significance of this being plain. Female monkeys also exercise some choice of males; they prefer to present to particular individuals and make themselves very unavailable to others. Therefore, there is some selection taking place between males as well as between females, though for males the criteria focus more on skills and prowess than on appearance.

A similar state of affairs prevails with humans. Men choose their mates primarily according to visual attributes; women select according to intelligence, achievement and other characteristics associated with social class. This means that physical beauty is upwardly mobile particularly for women, while talent and ability is more advantageous for men. Good looks and high intelligence therefore tend to accrue within the higher classes since both are marketable commodities. For example, a recent study showed that fat legs in women is a characteristic that results in downward class mobility both within and between generations; dietary differences between the classes were not sufficient to explain the observations. Extreme ugliness or mental deficiency in either sex may result not just in lowered class position, but in total failure to attract a mate and reproduce. The important social function served by prostitutes is clear when it is realised that they may be the only sexual outlet for some of the most severely disadvantaged individuals.

In most societies, including our own, it is the males who are supposed to take the initiative in approaching a mate. To this end they employ a variety of techniques – songs, poems, letters, gifts, love-charms, and so on. Very seldom do they solicit intercourse overtly by verbal request or physical assault. Females also exercise considerable influence in the process, despite the contrary rule about male initiative. They have the option of accepting or rejecting the overtures from the different men, but they also manage to find subtle ways of showing interest in particular men and communicating a readiness to make love with them. Parallel with monkeys, women tend to become sexually assertive at particular times and are thus more variable than men in the degree of initiative shown. Finally, there is a tendency for males to show greater initiative in the early states of a relationship after which they appear to become satiated and lethargic and initiative is progressively taken over by the female – a pattern that is also apparent in both apes and other mammals as well as humans. Overall, women initiate about as much sexual activity as men and this is not a recent evolutionary development.

Love as a form of imprinting
Ducks and many other birds show a striking tendency to follow the first moving object that greets their eyes after hatching. This highly inflexible 'one-off' kind of learning is called *imprinting*. Higher animals including primates also show imprinting in early infancy; human babies for instance usually attach themselves firmly and persistently to a particular toy, blanket, or piece of cloth which they become dependent upon for comfort and security. Substitutes are not acceptable to the child unless they are so similar as to be indistinguishable from the original. This type of learning takes place only at critical periods of development, though not always in early infancy. It occurs at a discrete moment in time and is thereafter little affected by rewards or punishments. The acquisition of language, food fads, musical taste, and many other preferences seems to involve some of the characteristics of imprinting.

Certain idiosyncratic sexual fixations also appear to originate as a sort of one-shot conditioning process. The anthropologist Paul

Gebhard gives the example of a man who at puberty 'became involved in a childhood tussle with a girl somewhat larger and more powerful than he. While struggling and wriggling beneath her, he experienced not only his first conscious sexual arousal but in strong degree. This one experience has dominated his life ever since. He has continued to be attracted to large, muscular, dominant females; and in his hetero-sexual contacts he tries to arrange the same wrestling. He has, not surprisingly, developed some additional masochistic attributes.'

There is an increasing consensus among clinicians and researchers that imprinting-type processes may be involved in the origins of many perversions such as fetishism, exhibitionism, voyeurism, masochism, and transvestism. New Zealand sexologist John Money suggests that some people are imprinted on a homosexual love object at a critical point in their sexual development and others to a heterosexual love object. 'The existence of an early imprinting period would explain why an adolescent or adult, safely past the critical period, can be forced or induced into an aberrant sexual experience without becom-ing a chronic practitioner of that experience. Thus an occasional adult homosexual act does not produce homosexual imprinting.'

If abnormal sex objects can be imprinted, then of course normal objects should imprint all the more easily. Money believes that sex identity is imprinted some time between the ages of one and four; at a very young age the child makes an irrevocable decision as to whether it is male or female. The critical period for falling in love occurs some time after the onset of adolescence. The unfortunate teenager is a victim of all sorts of infatuations, many of them quite unrealistic. Any of these would be capable of developing into a mature romance given appropriate circumstances − reciprocation, social encouragement, and all the factors that have been discussed in this chapter and in chapter 4 (sex, caring, vicarious status, arousal, and so on). Such imprinting is not quite so inflexible as that seen in ducklings, but it does appear as slightly unreasonable and it is exclusive in that it precludes falling in love with anyone else at the same time.

An important facilitator of falling-in-love imprinting is freshness. Edward Brecher in his book *The Sex Researchers* notes that 'a rare thirteen-year old may fall in love with the boy or girl next door; much more commonly it is the new girl in town who discovers to her own amazement that she has become simultaneously the love object of half the boys in town. Whether this freshness requirement is one of the reasons for the relative rarity of incestuous falling-in-love experi-ences is a matter for speculation.' Given the genetic advantages of mating outside one's own family it is probably just as well that familiarity breeds contempt in this respect.

When the time is ripe we may well fall in love with somebody at first sight. It has even been known for people to fall in love without ever having met, for example with a film actress, or with the fantasy of a person that one is anticipating meeting. The syndrome of intense, passionate preoccupation that follows is well documented by poets and novelists. Anthropologists assure us that it is widespread – in time and place. Although it precludes falling in love with another individual at the same time, the spurned lover is usually able to fall in love again with somebody else later, after the previous experience has extinguished. However, after the first big experience in adolescence, it may never be quite so intense again and, if a couple have stayed together since then, extramarital affairs are unlikely to result in the same imprinting.

Imprinting, then, seems to be another important evolutionary basis for human love. It is a particularly important concept for explaining the unpredictability of love and the narrowness of its target, i.e. the 'Cupid's dart' nature of its visitations. The nurturant and comfort-seeking tendencies derived from the parent–child caring pattern can be satisfied to a greater or lesser extent by a wide variety of human and even non-human contacts (e.g. dolls, pets, and cushions). Exchange of favours, skills, conversation, and so on, are friendly processes that may occur with any person, male or female. The sexual pleasure exchange is restricted to certain types of people, usually the opposite sex, though a progressive reinforcement schedule tends to be set up with one particular partner. Imprinting, however, always takes place with one unique person – or at least one at a time. Operating in concert, these predispositions that we have inherited from our animal ancestors may be capable of producing the dramatic phenomenon that we identify as adult, human, romantic love.

10

The future of love

Visions of love in the future have focused on the way in which technology might replace interpersonal relationships. In films such as *Barbarella* and Woody Allen's *Sleeper*, people are electrically or chemically stimulated in a way so totally satisfying that it becomes a substitute for conventional love and sex. This has the advantages that it wastes less time and does not require the cooperation of another person. Other predictions of love emphasise political developments. In *Rollerball*, for example, the Corporate Society provides attractive partners for specified durations as a form of reward for services rendered to society. Again, it is presumed that the mystique of interpersonal relationships has been transcended or lost.

Science fiction in the past has often proved uncannily accurate in predicting the present. Do these films really show us the way that love and romance will have gone by the twenty-first century? Technology and politics are two important influences that have to be considered in extrapolating social trends. The other major factor, which can be viewed as a kind of homeostatic (stabilising) force, is human nature. In previous chapters we have looked at sexual attraction and love as they occur today, and tried to say how such behaviour in these areas reflects basic human nature and how much is due to transitory social pressures and conditions. Now we attempt to combine observations of ongoing technological and political developments with what we have learned about the psychology of love, to arrive at some informed guesses as to what the future may hold.

The age of permissiveness
The last few decades have seen an astonishing trend towards permissive sexual attitudes in the West. Few would question that we are now much more frank and open about sexual matters than we were a few years ago — television, newspapers, magazines and conversations are generally much more explicit.

Although it has sometimes been denied, there have also been

The age of first intercourse is declining

	Born	
	1943–1944	**1953–54**
Age 15 years or less	4% boys	10% boys
	1% girls	7% girls
Age 16 years or less	7% boys	38% boys
	3% girls	26% girls

The apparent trend towards initiation in sexual activities at a younger age was confirmed in a recent German survey. The proportion of boys and girls who had experienced intercourse by the age of 15 or 16 years increased markedly over the ten years shown above. (from Schmidt and Sigusch 1972) changes in actual behaviour. Studies in several Western countries have shown increases in premarital and extramarital sex activity combined with decreases in associated guilt and remorse. For example, one study in Germany found that 7 per cent of boys and 3 per cent of girls born in 1943–4 had experienced intercourse by the age of 16, compared to 38 per cent of boys and 26 per cent of girls born ten years later in 1953–4. This is a striking change towards younger initiation to the joys of sex and it is paralleled by higher incidences of nearly every kind of sexual behaviour that has been classified as immoral in the past. The survey results may partly reflect increased honesty, but it is also clear that behaviour has been changing in the permissive direction apart from willingness to report it.

How much further do we expect this trend to continue, and is there likely to be a counter revolution at some time in the future? A popular idea is that sexual morality follows historical cycles, waxing and waning like the ice ages. Proponents of this view argue that present permissiveness is merely a reaction against repressive Victorianism and that we can soon expect the pendulum to start returning.

Analysis of the probable causes of the present trend suggests that this is not the case. Although we can expect some minor reactions from time to time, e.g. the recent Festival of Light campaign in Britain, permissiveness will probably continue to increase generally for some time yet, until a new equilibrium is reached. It is impossible to say for sure what the main causes are, but some of the factors associated with permissiveness are

1 The breakdown of religious beliefs and values, removing fears of divine retribution
2 Improved communication and transportation, resulting in greater experience of cultural diversity
3 Population increase and urbanisation, leading to increased anonymity and a greater range of transitory encounters
4 Increased prosperity, bringing more leisure time and greater economic freedom
5 Availability of convenient and effective birth control measures, reducing the fear of pregnancy
6 Other inventions such as cars and films which have resulted in increased experience and opportunity for casual sexual encounters

Most of these scientific, technological and social changes are not readily reversible, so there is no reason to expect that the permissiveness which they have promoted will be reversed either. It would be difficult to forget that Charles Darwin ever wrote *Origin of Species*, difficult to revert to traditional village life, and difficult to ban television, cars and contraceptives. Yet something of the kind would probably have to occur if we are ever going to revert to puritanism or Victorianism. Permissiveness is very firmly established because its root causes are in scientific advances that are unlikely to be abandoned.

Natural brakes on promiscuity

Science has removed many of the inhibitions against random sexual encounters, but others are left. One is venereal disease. Syphilis is now fairly well controlled but gonorrhoea and some other kinds are on the increase. This, however, is another draw-back that we would expect science to relieve us of in the future.

Are there any restrictions on promiscuity that we would not expect to disappear as a result of technological advances or religious-moral relaxations? If there are they must reside within the psychology of human beings. It is our belief that there are built-in reservations (character traits such as modesty, shyness, or reticence) which militate against random sexual matings. The animal and cross-cultural studies described in the previous chapter suggest that females in particular are careful about when they engage in sex, and with whom. They display distinct reservation until the time is right, and in animals anyway this is not due to religious or moral ideology. Presumably, female primates have evolved more caution about sexual contacts because they have more at stake socially and biologically. Not only do they carry a greater burden of responsibility for seeing that they are in a position to care for offspring when they arrive, but the genetic constitution of the next generation is in their control. For a male animal sex can be just a bit of fun; females have to live with the repercussions. Of course, subhumans are not able to weigh things up consciously as we do, which is precisely why instinctual mechanisms underlying reserved social and sexual behaviour have been evolved. Probably neither women or men are promiscuous by nature; both sexes are selective to an extent, and incline towards moderately lasting bonds.

Apart from biologically based reservations, there are many good social reasons for caution in choosing sexual contacts which fairly inevitably find their way into our psychology. Jealousy is a very basic human emotion, even if certain individuals and groups have succeeded in controlling it at times. Without some semblance of stability in interpersonal relationships, sexual and non-sexual, a great deal of insecurity is bound to arise. Promiscuity is largely incompatible with either romantic or companionate love, and the human need for these understandings will continue to act as a kind of brake on partner turnover.

.Unfortunately monogamy is not really in our nature either. In chapter 8 we described the need for excitement and novelty that we all have to some extent, especially men. This means that a conflict between novelty seeking and jealousy avoidance is an inevitable product of human nature and no easy solution to it is envisaged in the future.

Social pressure goes both ways
The inhibitory effects of social norms upon sexual behaviour are very obvious since we have so recently emerged from a particularly repressive era. But social pressures can push *towards* promiscuity as well as away from it. If your friends and neighbours all join the local swinging club you might well feel under some pressure to participate also, even though your emotional inclination goes against it. If the media lay undue emphasis on extreme and kinky kinds of sex because this draws audiences (perhaps more out of curiosity than anything else) it can amount to a social pressure to conform by experimenting with sexual behaviour that would not otherwise have been contemplated. It would be easy to feel dull, undersexed or 'square' if one did not engage in the activities constantly depicted by the media.

Another possible example of a reversal in the direction of social pressure is the effects of the Women's Liberation movement. In the past, and perhaps still today, social pressures have prevented women considering certain careers. Society has dictated that they become housewives rather than engineers, nurses rather than doctors, and so on. Now a reverse propaganda campaign has been launched. Schoolbooks which show occupational sex differences are being withdrawn, women are being persuaded to enter previously male occupations, and there is pressure upon men to share tasks such as housekeeping and child care. Although it may not have gone so far yet, it is entirely possible that a political movement of this kind could run us counter to nature in the opposite direction. Women who would have preferred the roles of housewife and mother might be pressured into behaviour they did not really enjoy or be made to feel failures as a result of this campaign.

Even their sex lives might suffer. Birmingham (England) sex therapist Dr Philip Cauthery believes that men are beginning to retreat from women sexually. Dropping rates of marital intercourse are reported along with increases in masturbation by married men. Although this may be due to changes in willingness to report the different activities, or to an increase in extramarital intercourse, Cauthery argues that increased female assertiveness has led to a kind of mental emasculation of modern husbands. The current witch-hunt for chauvinists could have damaged the male ego in a way that has reacted to the detriment of the female sex life. If men are afraid to assert themselves for fear of female rejection, the sexual fulfilment of both men and women may be impaired.

Social pressure, then, is not always of a conservative kind. Sometimes it pushes people towards behaviour that is more radical than their natural inclination. If such a point is reached with respect to sexual promiscuity and perversions we might well witness a slight reversion in the direction of traditional morality before the end of the century, though a return to Victorianism proper is not a real prospect.

Love after the sexual revolution

Will the trend towards uninhibited sexual behaviour have any effect upon manifestations of romantic love? Some have suggested that love will disappear completely and sex will be reduced to a mechanical, though still pleasurable, act. This prediction is based on the idea that love is in some way dependent upon restricted and exclusive sexual liaisons.

Comparison of the most sexually liberated parts of the world, such as Denmark and California, with relatively conservative corners such as Spain and Tennessee, does not suggest any major breakdown of love as a result of excessive permissiveness; nor does comparison of the liberal and conservative elements within any one area. However, no formal research of this kind has been done, and it could be argued that the trend has a long way to go yet, so we will have to await further developments before we can say with any certainty that permissiveness does not destroy love.

What would be predicted on the basis of the theories of love outlined in this book? The attribution theory implies that passionate love is fired by jealousy as well as any other emotion, so perhaps it will thrive in permissive conditions. However, attribution theory also says that sexual frustration and sexual excitement are important facilitators of love. If sex is easily obtainable, frustration would not occur so frequently and excitement would be less because the novelty would have worn off to some extent. On this basis we might expect romantic love to occur less often and with less intensity. The ethological theory that love bonds are reinforced by sexual gratification between two persons would also suggest that love would be spread thinner if sex is had with several different people simultaneously. The sum total of love might be about the same but romantic feelings towards each individual partner proportionately reduced.

Against these negatives some possible beneficial effects of permissiveness should be considered. One is removal of unpleasant emotions such as guilt, fear and disgust from sexual behaviour. These inhibitory feelings must have prevented many couples in the past from achieving any kind of sexual fulfilment, thus interfering with the development of love. Another positive gain might be the generalised contentment derived from a full sex life. A certain amount of human anger and bitterness might be drained away in the permissive society, leaving more fertile ground for the growth of all kinds of affection.

On balance, then, we might expect a slight dilution of love with increasing permissiveness, but by no means its total obliteration. Certain types of love, especially the passionate, manic kind may be somewhat diminished in intensity, but society will probably benefit from more widely spread love sentiments. Perhaps we are gradually moving from a condition in which sex served to consolidate two-person relationships only, into an era when it will help to promote social relations within a broader group. The recent slogan 'make love, not war' has a certain intuitive appeal to it, and the proponents of encounter groups and swinging claim to derive great feelings of comradeship with fellow group members from the experience. Perhaps, to date, we have been wasting the socialising and pacifying potential of sex by restricting it to two-person exclusive relationships.

Marriage and divorce
The future of marriage is a related and equally debated question. The recent trend has been for the marriage rate to hold up fairly well; as a legal institution it is not yet showing any signs of going out of fashion. There are, however, some striking changes in its nature. People are getting married for the first time at a younger age on average, they are getting married more times each, and more often at a registry office. The divorce rate in Britain has risen by over 200 per cent in the last decade, and similar increases have been noted in other Western countries. This means that a lot of today's marriages are actually remarriages, and since more people are remarrying without the marriage rate being inflated, more people must be managing to avoid the state altogether. In a sense, then, marriage *is* on the decline; more people get married several times, more people do not get married at all, and more people go through non-religious ceremonies.

The decline of traditional life-long marriage is related to factors very similar to those which have contributed to permissiveness in general. Religious and legal restrictions against divorce have been relaxed; there is greater population density and movement, more economic freedom, and greater opportunity to experiment with extramarital relations. There is no reason to think that these trends will not continue for some years to come. The full effects of birth control have yet to be seen, religion is likely to retreat further as a moral force, and there will be still more leisure time in the future. As the rate of divorce increases, and the ease with which it can be obtained, a point will be reached where the legal institution of marriage collapses in the same way that the religious institution has already largely done. At some stage young couples are going to ask themselves why they should take on unnecessary legal commitments in addition to all the other problems involved in setting up home together.

As with the decline of religious morality, freedom from marital ties will have much less effect on human mating behaviour than many people think, because of the psychological bonds that stabilise relationships between men and women. First there is the love bond which we have discussed many times in this book. It is a real thing, not just a Hollywood myth, and it has power to keep a couple together for a reasonable (if variable) period of time without bolstering by religious or legal pressures. A second bond is mutual love of the children produced by the relationship. By the time the first bond has withered, the second has usually come into operation. Although one or both of the partners may by this time have acquired romantic leanings elsewhere, neither wants to give up the children, so even in the absence of marital ties they would often choose to continue living together on a companionate basis. If they do not claim property rights on each other such as those implied by traditional marriage, they are freer to develop satisfying relationships with other people and can probably live together much more amicably as a result. A lot of couples might live monogamous lives with their first loves, but they will do so by volition rather than compulsion. Thus, abandoning traditional marriage, as we are slowly doing, should increase the amount of 'true love' to be found in the world.

The trend towards open marriage that we predict implies a severing, or at least weakening, of the link between romantic love and marriage as a social institution concerned with the provision and care of children. The fairy tale and Hollywood ideology, which is still frequently promulgated by the media and well-intentioned parents, is that passionate love is the sole necessary basis on which to select someone with whom to live happily ever after. But of course, this kind of love is inclined to be transitory, whereas the social responsibilities incurred are very long-lasting. Probably the future will see a cancellation of the equation between love and marriage and a move towards rational couplings. Romantic love will cease to be viewed as an essential basis on which to found a family, with the result that children will be better cared for and middle aged couples will live together more happily because they are better suited to each other. At the same time, an easing of restrictions against non-marital love relationships will allow sexual love to flourish independently.

Partner selection

If partner choice is to become increasingly rational in the future, does this mean that computer dating bureaux will have a greater contribution to make? Possibly yes, but they will need to acquire more sophistication as regards the factors taken into account in the matching. Research such as that described in chapter 3 will assist in the process, but a great deal more will have to be done before we will really be in a position to say what personality and other combinations are most favourable. Among the additional details that could be stored by the computer are medical details of genetically transferable

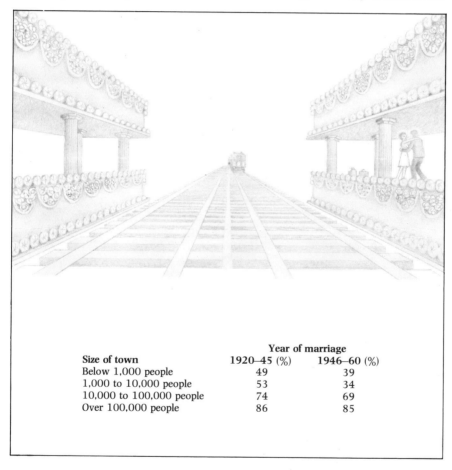

Size of town	Year of marriage	
	1920–45 (%)	1946–60 (%)
Below 1,000 people	49	39
1,000 to 10,000 people	53	34
10,000 to 100,000 people	74	69
Over 100,000 people	86	85

Nowadays we are less likely to marry someone from our home town

As people become more mobile, they are more likely to seek a partner outside their home town. The above results were obtained in a British survey which revealed that the proportion of people marrying within their home town has declined since 1920.

(from Population Investigation Committee survey; cited by Coleman 1973) diseases. In this way people could avoid meeting, and therefore mating, with others carrying the same recessive defects, and their children would be healthier as a result. The alternative, of course, is to live with someone psychologically compatible, and have children with someone genetically compatible, making use of techniques such as artificial insemination.

A type of research that has widespread implications for issues such as inbreeding and the future of a population, is how married couples meet in the natural course of events. David Coleman, an anthropologist from London University, summarised the pattern that has emerged for Britain as follows:

> If a man lives in an average-sized town, he will probably marry a girl from the same town, who was also born there. The odds are higher if he has a working class rather than a middle class background. He is very unlikely to marry the girl next door. Probably the couple will meet at the local Top Rank palais de dance, without their families ever having met before. However, he is much more likely than his father to find a girl living far away.

The tendency to look further afield for a partner is likely to increase in the future. A survey in Britain showed that fewer people married within their home town in the fifties than twenty years earlier; the decrease for small towns was from 49 per cent to 39 per cent. Probably the most important reason for this is increasing mobility, which has resulted from car-ownership and increasing affluence. In one survey, the average distance travelled each day was 11·9 miles in 1968, compared with only 6·3 miles in 1953. Individuals travel further for their entertainment; in particular those from small towns travel to larger towns because of the attraction of amenities such as dance halls and clubs. As contact between towns increases, so does the opportunity for marriages between people living further away from each other.

A population implosion?

One of the most significant technological advances relevant to sex and love is modern birth control, especially the pill and intra-uterine device. No doubt further advances are ahead of us, but we are only just beginning to see the effects that this innovation will have on sexual behaviour and population growth. For the first time in history we are free to determine the course of our own evolution by separating sexual pleasure from reproduction.

The Catholic Church has always resisted this separation of sex from reproduction. It is not clear why – perhaps because pleasure is equated with sin, or because such an attitude is good for the survival of the religion because it keeps up the numbers. But the Catholic insistence on reproduction as the sole function of sex is clearly wrong in view of the evolution of human love described in the last chapter. In humans, sex serves the higher purpose of promoting love between the couple so they will want to stay together and take care of their offspring. The simple copulation-reproduction sequence is a characteristic of lower animals. It is ironic that the religion which fought so hard against the Darwinian suggestion that men are basically animals should at this late stage in history continue to debase man's sexuality.

Great fear has been expressed about the current population explosion. Indeed, it has reached terrible proportions. Science, which was largely responsible for it in the first place by improving health and medicine and thus increasing life expectancy, may not have come up with effective birth control measures quite in time. But if we do survive the next few over-crowded decades we might then have to concern ourselves with a drastically declining population.

The reason for thinking this is that humans do not appear to have any instinct for generating children *per se*. All that is biologically necessary for survival of a species (at least those that are not clever enough to invent birth control) is a sex drive which impels it to copulate, and a parental instinct which ensures that it cares for the resulting offspring. A built-in need to produce children is biologically superfluous if the animal is not aware of the connection between coitus and pregnancy, or can do nothing to stop it.

There are increasing signs today that people do not naturally set out to make babies at a high rate. A large percentage of babies in the past were accidentally conceived and very few were actively sought. With birth control only just becoming widespread, the birth rate in most Western countries including Britain and the United States has already fallen to about the replacement level. With society changing its emphasis from a glamorised view of pregnancy and child-birth to a more realistic portrayal, and with growing propaganda about the social responsibility not to contribute further to the population explosion, the birth rate might fall well below replacement.

At the moment there is an overpopulation problem, and the world as a whole is approaching disaster point. But the problem is coming from the underdeveloped parts of the world, especially Asia, not the advanced Western countries. Our local problem, if we survive the world's problem, could well be the exact reverse – that of a population 'implosion'.

The increasing importance of attractiveness
As society becomes more urbanised and mobile we are seeing an in-

crease in the number of transitory encounters with people – the girl we talk to on the train on the way to work, the man who slices ham in the supermarket, the proprietor of the motel we stay in overnight, and so on. This increase in the extent to which meetings are brief and superficial should lead to an increased value attached to physical attractiveness. After all, people do not get a chance to appreciate our many other virtues; they hardly see us long enough to provide the police with an adequate description should we have raped them or stolen their watch.

Attractiveness is most important in those (typically urban) jobs that involve brief contact with a high turnover of people, e.g. air hostess, receptionist and salesperson (aside from explicitly decorative occupations such as model and chorus girl). Hence we see a lot of advertisements which blatantly solicit attractive people. Complaints against this discrimination have already been heard, and an 'Uglies Liberation' movement has appeared in the United States. The success of this political enterprise has so far been limited, but we should resist the temptation to ridicule the case in view of the impressive gains made by other liberation movements in recent decades.

The counter argument is that only attractive people would want these jobs and be comfortable in them. It has even been suggested that they are ideal for people whose prime or only attribute is attractiveness. Such people can be afforded fairly instantaneous respect in jobs like this without any need to sustain it for long periods of time. People of lesser attractiveness would be less likely to enjoy a job that involved only superficial acquaintance with a lot of people. They would prefer jobs in which they could develop long-term personal relationships with a limited number of people, e.g. school teacher, farm worker or research scientist. The future will probably see an increasing tendency for people to gravitate towards different occupations according to their physical attractiveness.

Aids to beauty

Given the increasing importance of attractiveness in modern fluid society, the next few decades will also see increased use of a great variety of beauty aids. These will range from medical developments like diet pills, hormone therapy, and face lift operations to special exercise programmes and advanced cosmetics. With increasing sexual equality men will probably use cosmetics a great deal more than previously.

Many film stars undergo plastic surgery to improve their looks, as do people with unfortunate features such as an exceptionally large nose. Occasional problems relating to a partial loss of identity have been reported, but in general the effects have been very beneficial to the person's subsequent life.

The effect of giving plastic surgery to disfigured criminals was studied by Richard Kurtzberg and colleagues in the New York area. They selected a large group of disfigured prisoners, and upon their release gave some of them plastic surgery, some vocational guidance, and some both. A follow-up investigation one year later showed that the recidivism rate of those given surgery was 36 per cent less than those given no help. Vocational guidance also proved useful, but only when it had been given in conjunction with cosmetic surgery. Treatment was also shown to be more helpful to those with facial disfigurements than those with body disfigurements, which strengthens the argument that an improvement in outward beauty was responsible for the reduction in criminal activity.

Although the cost of plastic surgery is high, it can be considered negligible compared with the cost of keeping people in jail for a number of years (not just the economics, but the human suffering involved). Likewise, it has been suggested that plastic surgery might sometimes be considered as an adjunct to psychotherapy. For example, if an ugly girl seeks psychotherapy because she feels lonely and rejected and is unable to find a boy friend, she might well be advised to consider plastic surgery. The time and expense required by this approach could hardly exceed that of engaging a psychotherapist to help her to live with her problem.

Pleasure machines
Are other people really necessary for gratification? Could they be replaced entirely by private forms of pleasure? The possibility does not seem quite so remote and silly today as it would have done thirty years or so ago.

In 1954 Michigan psychologist James Olds was studying the way rats responded to passing tiny electric currents into various parts of their brain when he made an interesting discovery. When the electrode was placed in an area of the mid-brain called the limbic system the rat showed signs of wanting more. It would return repeatedly to the part of the cage in which the stimulus had first been received, and if stimulation was only given when the rat was located in a particular part of the cage it would eventually stay there without moving. The next step was to provide the rat with a key which would enable him to close the circuit and deliver an electrical current to himself; in this set-up he was observed to press the key feverishly. The areas of the brain that lend themselves to this self-stimulation phenomenon have come to be called 'pleasure areas' and they have since been demonstrated in many other animals including humans.

Neuropsychologists believe that any pleasurable sensation we experience, whether due to an orgasm, a musical symphony, a field of daffodils, or roast turkey, is perceived as enjoyable because these pleasure areas have been neurologically activated somehow or another. If that is so, why not short circuit the process and plug in to direct pleasure? After all, it seems only one step further along a line of vicariousness from watching television. Drugs such as mescaline and LSD also seem to be capable of evoking pure pleasure sensations, perhaps because they act chemically on the pleasure areas in a manner somewhat parallel to electrical stimulation.

It is likely that these direct sources of pleasure will some day come to be more socially acceptable than they are today. At the moment society is very wary of them, fearing that they might spell the end of human civilisation. Only a few years ago, Harvard psychologist Timothy Leary was imprisoned for openly advocating the widespread use of hallucinogens for recreation and 'mind-expansion'. Society is naturally enough repelled by the prospect of everybody being constantly 'spaced out' on some kind of orgasmic 'trip', with nobody doing any work or accepting responsibility. Obviously, this would be self-destructive in the long run.

Humans who have received stimulation of their pleasure areas (usually mental patients) report a variety of pleasurable experiences, e.g. 'feeling great', imminent orgasm, drunkenness and elimination of bad thoughts. Given control of their own stimulation they go on pressing the switch in a compulsive manner. To the observer, this is reminiscent of an addiction — like the chain smoker who goes on lighting cigarettes or the alcoholic who goes on pouring drinks. However, in the case of pleasure centre stimulation no anger or withdrawal effects are observed when the current is cut off. As with drugs like mescaline, there is memory of the pleasurable experience but no desperate craving to repeat it comparable to nicotine or heroin addiction.

Despite the obvious advantages of these direct pleasure experiences, we doubt that they will ever completely replace the more sociable forms of gratification. We have probably evolved in such a way that the ultimately subtle pleasures are those obtained from interaction with our environment, and especially contact with other people in it. However far the techniques of self-stimulation are developed, we will still need to interact with other people and we will still wish to feel autonomous in our behaviour; therefore we will continue to hate and love and feel the complete range of human emotions. We may occasionally plug in to masturbatory machines of one sort or another, and we may occasionally use direct stimulation of the pleasure areas to enhance our interpersonal relationships, but we will never completely submit control of our experiences to drugs and electrodes. The human race is too proud and too wise to do that.

Tolerance of variety

One other general trend that we expect to see is an increasing differentiation of attitudes and behaviour in connection with love and sex. Hopefully this will be paralleled by increased tolerance of diversity.

As society becomes more advanced and urbanised there is call for a greater variety of talents and specialisations. One person becomes a

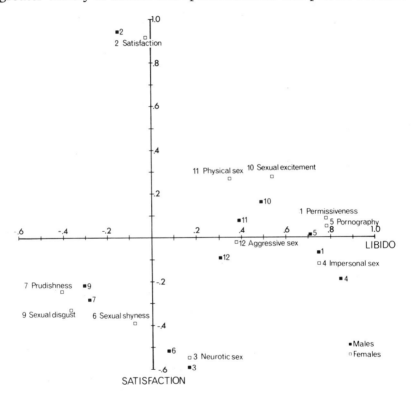

Satisfaction does not depend on sex drive

The questionnaire and genetic studies of Hans Eysenck have led to the conclusion that individual differences in sexual attitudes and behaviour can be described in terms of two major dimensions, labelled Libido versus Restraint and Satisfaction versus Pathology. Because these dimensions are found to be independent we have a situation whereby people expressing satisfaction with their sex life may be either 'monogamous puritans' at one extreme or 'happy philanderers indulging in wine, women and song' at the other extreme. Moreover, because these types are so firmly established, it is unlikely that social pressures could change one type into the other.

(from Eysenck 1976)

computer technician, others become architects, astronauts, cartoonists, psychoanalysts, and so on. Such occupational differentiation leads to markedly differing life styles, hence different attitudes and preferences. Inevitably we come to accept and appreciate these differences. We no longer expect everyone to behave in accordance with a single norm.

We also have increasingly clear evidence of a biological basis to the variations in sexual appetite displayed by different people. This applies not just to the average difference between men and women, but to the more striking differences between individuals within each sex. For example, the twin studies of Hans Eysenck revealed that two-thirds of the variation in male libidos was due to heredity. Eysenck also found that the degree of satisfaction with their sex life expressed by different people was unconnected with either their libido or the permissiveness of their attitudes. Clearly, there are no rational grounds for insisting that people follow one life-style rather than another. Either chastity or promiscuity, or an intermediate course, can lead to happiness, depending on the biological nature of the individuals concerned.

In modern California, one of the most advanced, affluent and diversified of societies, an incredible range of life styles is offered — everything from the puritanical to the frankly promiscuous. The amazing thing is that for the most part they exist side by side in reasonable harmony. In fact, whenever large numbers of people from divergent backgrounds live within a limited geographical area they must eventually learn to accept their biological and cultural differences and cater for them. If not, they cannot survive.

This civilised 'cosmopolitanism' is surely the way of the future. We will be forced to accept and tolerate many different types of loving and marital arrangements — homosexual pairings, threesomes, communes, swinging clubs, dial-a-prostitute services, and pleasure machines. We will even have to tolerate male–female couples who wish to engage in nothing but monogamous, orthodox sex, and individuals who wish to remain chaste for their entire lives.

Here is the distinction between promiscuity and permissiveness. Promiscuity is just one form of sexual behaviour offered by permissive society, and probably one that is selected only by a minority. Permissiveness means acceptance of the fact that people differ, both biologically and in terms of their experiences, and tolerance of the various forms of love-making and living arrangements that they arrive at as a result. In this sense we hope that the trend towards permissiveness will never be arrested.

Reading list

This book is based on material from numerous sources. Some of the journal articles and books upon which we relied most heavily are listed below.

Chapter 1

BERSCHEID, E. and WALSTER, E. H. *Interpersonal Attraction* (Reading, Massachusetts, 1969: Addison-Wesley)

BERSCHEID, E. and WALSTER, E. H. 'Physical attractiveness', in L. Berkowitz (ed.), *Advances in Experimental Social Psychology*, volume 7 (New York, 1975: Academic Press)

DION, K. K. 'Physical attractiveness and evaluation of children's transgressions', *Journal of Personality and Social Psychology* 24 (1972), 207–13

DION, K., BERSCHEID, E. and WALSTER, E. 'What is beautiful is good', *Journal of Personality and Social Psychology* 24 (1972), 285–90

HUSTON, T. L. (ed.) *Foundations of Interpersonal Attraction* (New York, 1974: Academic Press)

KIRKPATRICK, C. and COTTON, J. 'Physical attractiveness, age, and marital adjustment', *American Sociological Review* 16 (1951), 81–6

LANDY, D. and SIGALL, H. 'Beauty is talent: task evaluation as a function of the performer's physical attractiveness', *Journal of Personality and Social Psychology* 29 (1974), 299–304

MATHES, E. W. and KAHN, A. 'Physical attractiveness, happiness, neuroticism, and self-esteem', *Journal of Psychology* 90 (1975), 27–30

MILLER, A. G. 'Role of physical attractiveness in impression formation', *Psychonomic Science* 19 (1970), 241–3

SIGALL, H. and LANDY, D. 'Radiating beauty: effects of having a physically attractive partner on person perception', *Journal of Personality and Social Psychology* 28 (1973), 218–24

SIGALL, H. and OSTROVE, N. 'Beautiful but dangerous: effects of offender attractiveness and nature of the crime on juridic judgment', *Journal of Personality and Social Psychology* 31 (1975), 410–14

WILSON, G. D. and BRAZENDALE, A. H. 'Sexual attractiveness, social attitudes and response to risqué humour', *European Journal of Social Psychology* 3 (1973), 95–6

Chapter 2

CAVIOR, N. 'Physical attractiveness, perceived attitude similarity, and interpersonal attraction among fifth and eleventh grade boys and girls', Ph.D. thesis, University of Houston, 1970

GALTON, F. *Inquiries into Human Faculty and its Development* (London, 1883: Macmillan)

HESS, E. H. 'Attitude and pupil size', *Scientific American* 212 (1965), 46–54

ILIFFE, A. H. 'A study of preferences in feminine beauty', *British Journal of Psychology* 51 (1960), 267–73

KOPERA, A. A., MAIER, R. A. and JOHNSON, J. E. 'Perception of physical attractiveness', *Proceedings of the 79th Annual Convention of the American Psychological Association* 6 (1971), 317–18

LAVRAKAS, P. 'Building a better man', *Behaviour Today* 6 (1975), 529

MATHEWS, A. M., BANCROFT, J. H. J. and SLATER, P. 'The principal components of sexual preference', *British Journal of Social and Clinical Psychology* 11 (1972), 35–43

MURSTEIN, B. I. 'Physical attractiveness and marital choice', *Journal of Personality and Social Psychology* 22 (1972), 8–12

SCODEL, A. 'Heterosexual somatic preference and fantasy dependency', *Journal of Consulting Psychology* 21 (1957), 371–4

WIGGINS, J. S., WIGGINS, N. and CONGER, J. C. 'Correlates of heterosexual somatic preference', *Journal of Personality and Social Psychology* 10 (1968), 82–90

WIGGINS, N. and WIGGINS, J. S. 'A typological analysis of male preferences for female body types', *Multivariate Behavioral Research* 4 (1969), 89–102

WILSON, G. D., NIAS, D. K. B. and BRAZENDALE, A. H. 'Vital statistics, perceived sexual attractiveness, and response to risqué humor', *Journal of Social Psychology* 95 (1975), 201–5

WILSON, P. R. 'Perceptual distortion of height as a function of ascribed academic status', *Journal of Social Psychology* 74 (1968), 97–102

Chapter 3

ARONSON, E. and LINDER, D. 'Gain and loss of esteem as determinants of interpersonal attractiveness', *Journal of Experimental Social Psychology* 1 (1965), 156–71

BERSCHEID, E., DION, K., WALSTER, E. and WALSTER, G. W. 'Physical attractiveness and dating choice: a test of the matching hypothesis', *Journal of Experimental Social Psychology* 7 (1971), 173–89

BYRNE, D. *The Attraction Paradigm* (New York, 1971: Academic Press)

BYRNE, D., ERVIN, C. R. and LAMBERTH, J. 'Continuity between the experimental study of attraction and real-life computer dating', *Journal of Personality and Social Psychology* 16 (1970), 157–65

BYRNE, D., LONDON, O. and REEVES, K. 'The effect of physical attractiveness, sex, and attitude similarity on interpersonal attraction', *Journal of Personality* 36 (1968), 259–71

CENTERS, R. 'The completion hypothesis and the compensatory dynamic in intersexual attraction and love', *Journal of Psychology* 82 (1972), 111–26

MILLER, A. R. 'Analysis of the Oedipal Complex', *Psychological Reports* 24 (1969), 781–2

MURSTEIN, B. I. 'Self–ideal-self discrepancy and the choice of marital partner', *Journal of Consulting and Clinical Psychology* 37 (1971), 47–52

NIAS, D. K. B. 'Personality and other factors determining the recreational interests of children and adults', Ph.D. thesis, University of London, 1975

SILVERMAN, I. 'Physical attractiveness and courtship', *Sexual Behavior* 7 (1971), 22–5

SINBERG, R. M., ROBERTS, A. F. and McCLAIN, D. 'Mate selection factors in computer matched marriages', *Journal of Marriage and the Family* 34 (1972), 611–14

TERMAN, L. M. *Psychological Factors in Marital Happiness* (New York, 1938: McGraw Hill)

TOUHEY, J. C. 'Effects of dominance and competence on heterosexual attraction', *British Journal of Social and Clinical Psychology* 13 (1974), 22–6

WALSTER, E. 'The effects of self-esteem on romantic liking', *Journal of Experimental Social Psychology* 1 (1965), 184–97

WALSTER, E., ARONSON, V., ABRAHAMS, D. and ROTTMANN, L. 'Importance of physical attractiveness in dating behaviour', *Journal of Personality and Social Psychology* 4 (1966), 508–16

Chapter 4

EYSENCK, H. J. *Fact and Fiction in Psychology* (London, 1965: Penguin)

DION, K. L. and DION, K. K. 'Correlates of romantic love', *Journal of Consulting and Clinical Psychology* 41 (1973), 51–6

DRISCOLL, R., DAVIS, K. E. and LIPETZ, M. E. 'Parental interference and romantic love: the Romeo and Juliet effect', *Journal of Personality and Social Psychology* 24 (1972), 1–10

DUTTON, D. G. and ARON, A. P. 'Some evidence for heightened sexual attraction under conditions of high anxiety', *Journal of Personality and Social Psychology* 30 (1974), 510–17

DUVALL, E. M. 'Adolescent love as a reflection of teen-agers' search for identity', in M. E. Lasswell and T. E. Lasswell (eds), *Love, Marriage, Family: A Developmental Approach* (Glenview, Illinois, 1973: Scott, Foresman)

KEPHART, W. M. 'Some correlates of romantic love', *Journal of Marriage and the Family* 29 (1967), 470–9

KIRKPATRICK, C. and CAPLOW, T. 'Courtship in a group of Minnesota students', *American Journal of Sociology* 51 (1945), 114–25

KNOX, D. H. 'Conceptions of love by married college students', *College Student Survey* 4 (1970), 28–30

KNOX, D. H. 'Attitudes toward love of high school seniors', *Adolescence* 5 (1970), 89–100

LEE, J. 'Styles of loving', *Psychology Today* (U.K. edition) 1 No 5 (August 1975), 20–7

RUBIN, Z. 'Measurement of romantic love', *Journal of Personality and Social Psychology* 16 (1970), 265–73

RUBIN, Z. *Liking and Loving: An Invitation to Social Psychology* (New York, 1973: Holt, Rinehart and Winston)

SCHACHTER, S. *The Psychology of Affiliation* (Stanford, California, 1969: Stanford University Press)

TENNOV, D. 'Sex differences in romantic love and depression among college students', *Proceedings of the 81st Annual Convention of the American Psychological Association* 8 (1973), 419–20

VALINS, S. 'Cognitive effects of false heart-rate feedback', *Journal of Personality and Social Psychology* 4 (1966), 400–8

WALSTER, E., WALSTER, G. W., PILIAVIN, J. and SCHMIDT, L. ' "Playing hard to get": understanding an elusive phenomenon', *Journal of Personality and Social Psychology* 26 (1973), 113–21

Chapter 5

COOPER, W. *No Change* (London, 1975: Hutchinson)

CORNER, G. W. 'Our knowledge of the menstrual cycle, 1910–1950', *Lancet* 1 (1951), 919–23

DOUST, J. W. L. and HUSZKA, L. 'Amines and aphrodisiacs in chronic schizophrenia', *Journal of Nervous and Mental Disease* 155 (1972), 261–4

EHRENKRANZ, J., BLISS, E. and SHEARD, M. H. 'Plasma testosterone: correlation with aggressive behaviour and social dominance in man', *Psychosomatic Medicine* 36 (1974), 469–75

ELLIS, A. and ABARBANEL, A. *The Encyclopedia of Sexual Behaviour*, volumes 1 and 2 (New York, 1961: Hawthorn)

GRAY, J. A. 'Sex differences in emotional behavior in mammals including man: endocrine bases', *Acta Psychologia* 35 (1971), 29–46

GREEP, R. O. and ASTWOOD, E. B. (eds), *Handbook of Physiology*, section 7, volume 2 (Washington, 1973: American Physiological Society)

McCLINTOCK, M. K. 'Menstrual synchrony and suppression', *Nature* 229 (1971), 244–5

MICHAEL, R. P., BONSALL, R. W. and WARNER, P. 'Human vaginal secretions: volatile fatty acid content', *Science* 186 (1974), 1217–19

REDGROVE, J. A. 'Menstrual cycles', in W. P. Colquhoun (ed.), *Biological Rhythms and Human Performance* (London, 1971: Academic Press)

SPITZ, C. J., GOLD, A. R. and ADAMS, D. B. 'Cognitive and hormonal factors affecting coital frequency', *Archives of Sexual Behavior* 4 (1975), 249–63

Chapter 6

BELL, A. P. 'Homosexualities: their range and character', in J. K. Cole and R. Dienstbier (eds), *1973 Nebraska Symposium on Motivation*, volume 21 (Lincoln, 1974: University of Nebraska)

HESTON, L. L. and SHIELDS, J. 'Homosexuality in twins: a family study and a registry study', *Archives of General Psychiatry* 18 (1968), 149–60

KALLMANN, F. J. 'Comparative twin study on the genetic aspects of male homosexuality', *Journal of Nervous and Mental Diseases* 115 (1952), 283–98

KINSEY, A. C., POMEROY, W. B. and MARTIN, C. E. *Sexual Behavior in the Human Male* (Philadelphia, 1948: Saunders)

KINSEY, A. C., POMEROY, W. B., MARTIN, C. E. and GEBHARD, P. H. *Sexual Behavior in the Human Female* (Philadelphia, 1953: Saunders)

KOLODNY, R. C., MASTERS, W. H., HENDRYX, J. and TORO, G. 'Plasma testosterone and semen analysis in male homosexuals', *New England Journal of Medicine* 285 (1971), 1170–4

LIEF, H. I., DINGMAN, J. F. and BISHOP, M. P. 'Psychoendrocrinologic studies in a male with cyclic changes in sexuality', *Psychosomatic Medicine* 24 (1962), 357–68

MONEY, J. *Sex Errors of the Body* (Baltimore, 1968: Johns Hopkins)

PRINCE, V. and BENTLER, P. M. 'Survey of 504 cases of transvestism', *Psychological Reports* 31 (1972), 903–17

RACHMAN, S. J. 'Sexual fetishism: an experimental analogue', *Psychological Record* 16 (1966), 293–6

SCHATZBERG, A. F., WESTFALL, M. P., BLUMETTI, A. B. and BIRK, C. L. 'Effeminacy: I. A quantitative rating scale', *Archives of Sexual Behavior* 4 (1975), 31–41

WAFELBAKKER, F. 'Marriage of homosexuals', *British Journal of Sexual Medicine* 2 (1975), 18–21

Chapter 7

BRECHER, E. M. *The Sex Researchers* (London, 1970: Deutsch)

BRECHER, R. and BRECHER, E. *An Analysis of Human Sexual Response* (Boston, 1966: Little, Brown)

DAVISON, G. C. and NEALE, J. M. *Abnormal Psychology: An Experimental Clinical Approach* (New York, 1975: Wiley)

FOX, C. A., WOLFF, H. and BAKER, J. A. 'Measurement of intra-vaginal and intra-uterine pressures during human coitus by radio telemetry', *Journal of Reproduction and Fertility* 22 (1970), 243–51

GILLAN, P. and GILLAN, R. *Sex Therapy Today* (London, 1976: Open Books)

KAPLIN, H. S. *The New Sex Therapy* (London, 1975: Balliere, Tindall and Cox)

MASTERS, W. H. and JOHNSON, V. E. *Human Sexual Response* (Boston, 1966: Little, Brown)

MASTERS, W. H. and JOHNSON, V. E. *Human Sexual Inadequacy* (Boston, 1970: Little, Brown)

MASTERS, W. H. and JOHNSON, V. E. *The Pleasure Bond* (New York, 1975: Bantam)

WRIGHT, H. *The Sex Factor in Marriage*, 5th ed. (London, 1966: Benn)

Chapter 8

BELL, R. R., TURNER, S. and ROSEN, L. 'A multivariate analysis of female extramarital coitus', *Journal of Marriage and the Family* 37 (1975), 375–84

EYSENCK, H. J. 'Personality and attitudes to sex: a factorial study', *Personality* 1 (1970), 355–76

SCHOFIELD, M. *The Sexual Behaviour of Young People* (London, 1965: Longman)

SMITH, J. R. and SMITH, L. G. 'Co-marital sex and the sexual freedom movement', *Journal of Sex Research* 6 (1970), 131–42

SPANIER, G. B. and COLE, C. L. 'Mate swapping: perceptions, value orientations, and participation in a midwestern community', *Archives of Sexual Behavior* 4 (1975), 143–59

SYMONDS, C. 'Sexual mate-swapping and the swingers', *Marriage Counseling Quarterly* 6 (1971), 1–12

THOMAS, D. R. 'Conservatism and premarital sexual experience', *British Journal of Social and Clinical Psychology* 14 (1975), 195–6

WILSON, G. D. (ed.) *The Psychology of Conservatism* (London, 1973: Academic Press)

WILSON, G. D. and NIAS, D. K. B. 'Sexual types: differences in attitudes and behaviour', *New Behaviour* 2 (1975), 330–2

Chapter 9

ARGYLE, M. *Social Interaction* (London, 1969: Methuen)

CLORE, G. L., WIGGINS, N. H. and ITKIN, S. 'Judging attraction from non-verbal behavior: the gain phenomenon', *Journal of Consulting and Clinical Psychology* 43 (1975), 491–7

DARWIN, C. R. *The Descent of Man and Selection in Relation to Sex* (London, 1883: Macmillan)

EIBL-EIBESFELDT, I. *Love and Hate: On the Natural History of Basic Behaviour Patterns* (London, 1971: Methuen)

FORD, C. S. and BEACH, F. A. *Patterns of Sexual Behavior* (New York, 1951: Harper)

HARLOW, H. F. 'The nature of love', *American Psychologist* 13 (1958), 673–85

HARLOW, H. F. and HARLOW, M. K. 'Social deprivation in monkeys', *Scientific American* 207 (1962), 137–46

MORRIS, D. *The Naked Ape* (London, 1967: Cape)

MORRIS, D. *Intimate Behaviour* (London, 1971: Cape)

SLUCKIN, W. *Imprinting and Early Learning* (London, 1964: Methuen)

WICKLER, W. 'Socio-sexual signals and their intra-specific imitation among primates', in D. Morris (ed.), *Primate Ethology* (London, 1967: Weidenfeld and Nicolson)

Chapter 10

CAMPBELL, H. J. *The Pleasure Areas* (London, 1973: Eyre Methuen)

COLEMAN, D. 'A geography of marriage', *New Society* 23 (1973), 634–6

EYSENCK, H. J. *Sex and Personality* (London, 1976: Open Books)

GORER, G. *Sex and Marriage in England Today* (London, 1971: Nelson)

KURTZBERG, R. L., SAFAR, H. and CAVIOR, N. 'Surgical and social rehabilitation of adult offenders', *Proceedings of the 76th Annual Convention of the American Psychological Association* 3 (1968), 649–50

LIGGETT, J. *The Human Face* (London, 1974: Constable)

SCHMIDT, G. and SIGUSCH, V. 'Changes in sexual behaviour among young males and females between 1960–1970', *Archives of Sexual Behaviour* 2 (1972), 27–45

WILSON, E. O. *Sociobiology; The New Synthesis* (Cambridge, Massachusetts, 1975: Belknap Press)

Index